His Eye Is On
The Sparrow

by **David and Ani Pearman**

Foreword by Jeffrey Hartensveld

Published by KHARIS PUBLISHING, an imprint of
KHARIS MEDIA LLC.

Copyright © 2024 David and Ani Pearman

ISBN-13: 978-1-63746-252-2

ISBN-10: 1-63746-252-2

Library of Congress Control Number:

Scripture quotations taken from the (NASB®) New American Standard
Bible®, Copyright ® 1960, 1971, 1977, 1995, by The Lockman Foundation.
Used by permission. All rights reserved. lockman.org

The Message: The Bible in Contemporary Language (MSG) is a translation of
the Bible in contemporary English. Authored by Eugene H. Peterson and
published in segments from 1993 to 2002 by NavPress.

All KHARIS PUBLISHING products are available at special quantity
discounts for bulk purchase for sales promotions, premiums, fund-raising,
and educational needs. For details, contact:

Kharis Media LLC
Tel: 1-630-909-3405
support@kharispublishing.com
www.kharispublishing.com

Praise for *His Eye is on the Sparrow*

Some stories which bring so much pain when they are lived, nonetheless bring so much healing when they are told. *His Eye is on the Sparrow* is one of those powerful, poignant stories. No child should have to endure what Dave Pearman endured. It is a testament to the strength of his character and courage, and especially to the providential grace and kindness of God, that Dave's hard journey, with all its twists and turns, is one that offers hope to the rest of us. This broken world, and maybe even your hurting heart, needs this healing story.

—**Jodi Detrick** DM, coach, mentor, speaker, author of *The Settled Soul* and *The Jesus-Hearted Woman*, former columnist for *The Seattle Times*

At a time when headlines are replete with misery and pain, this gripping, true story turns a narrative of suffering upside down, revealing hope. This riveting autobiography tells the story of an orphan who overcomes tragedy, trauma, and pain to become a successful husband, father, and businessman. Dave Pearman's story is the answer to the question: "Does God respond to human suffering?" Starting with the first chapter, this story will grab you, crush you, suck you in, and take you on a page-turning journey toward redemption and faith.

—**Rev. John W. Taylor**, lead pastor, Surabaya International Christian Assembly; director Sumba House of Hope

The story you are about to read is one of survival, determination and God's sovereignty. But maybe most important, it is a story of forgiveness. Dave Pearman's story will inspire you to forgive, to survive life's hardest times, and to know that God has a plan.

—**Rev. Jeff Hartensveld** DD, director, Asia Pacific, Assembly of God World Missions

David Pearman's inspiring story of an amazing life journey crosses cultural lines and shows how God's love transforms and heals in every situation. A "must read" book for anyone. I recommend it to everyone.

—**Rev. Dave Kenney**, Lead pastor, the International English Service (IES), Jakarta, Indonesia

There are few things more powerful than one's story, but a story like David's leads the reader toward hope and healing that changes lives. Read it, share it, and be inspired.

—**Dr. Eric Sandras** PhD, professor, recovery leader, author, TheDailySteps.com

Every journey takes us somewhere and we're never quite the person that we were at the beginning of that journey. *His Eye Is On The Sparrow* is a turning, twisting road towards the Journey Maker. It's a journey we are invited on by Joong Ki as he walks us through his early days of isolation, toughness, and stigma. It's a quest as Joong Ki becomes David Pearman and continues to take us toward a destination known by Him from the very beginning.

This story is strong, not only in the stark differences between the beginning and the end, but in the nuanced ways that changes come about and how "random" is really connected when we look back with David and see the dots joined together. *His Eye is on the Sparrow* is an invitation into David's life that also opens a window of reflection into our own lives. At the end of this memoir, you won't be the same person that you were beforehand, but you will know, in new and surprising ways, how His eye is on you too.

—**David Thomas**, training and curriculum director, EfeX English for Excellence, Surabaya, Indonesia

Dedication

The first and last person to Whom I owe my debt of gratitude is the Supreme Creator, our Father in Heaven, Who didn't leave me to die as an orphan. It is really His story of the Father's love in my life. Let this story lift up His name to every reader.

Acknowledgments

As I shared the initial part of my beginnings—or what I could recall— with a small group of Christians, they encouraged me to write down my story in a book. At the forefront of encouraging me was Jeff Hartensveld, the lead pastor at my international church in Surabaya, Indonesia. He invited me to tell my story of forgiveness to the entire church one Sunday. I also invited Pastor Jeff to be my Indonesian translator as I shared my story to my business staff and my wife's family. His Indonesian was as perfect as that of an Indonesian native speaker. It was quite a sight! He was a tall Caucasian person translating my talk, and I was a short Asian sharing my story—in English. The Indonesian waiters in the restaurant told other servers to come to the meeting room and watch this odd spectacle. They also were able to hear what Pastor Jeff translated out of my sharing.

Pastor Jeff would, on several occasions, urge, "Dave, when are you going to write your story? I will help you edit it. I know your story better than you!" He would eventually help me to have my pages edited and published.

There would be other friends who would encourage me along the way. For sure, this story of redemption could not be told if my mom and dad hadn't invited me as their son into their home with open, loving arms. Foremost, I need to acknowledge my wife, Ani, who believed my story could make a difference to many people. She tirelessly interviewed me, invested endless hours researching, and helped to write 80% of this manuscript. I'm positive my story would not be written completely if she hadn't been there alongside me.

Contents

Foreword

I met Dave Pearman in 2006 when he and his family began attending the international church my wife and I pastored in Surabaya, Indonesia. The Pearmans very quickly blended into our community and took on ministry responsibilities. They were and continue to be model Christians and church members. As our church grew and opened up branches around the city, we needed more preachers. In those days, the internet signal wasn't strong enough to live stream, so we went with a preaching team that would study together. We'd then co-produce a message and they preach it in different places. I opened a homiletics class on Friday nights to run concurrently with the youth group and I wasn't surprised when both Dave and Ani signed up for the class. During the semester of study we planned to culminate the end of the class by giving everyone in the class the chance to share a message. For the rest of my life I will never forget that night, because in Dave's message he shared a snippet of his life story. After hearing a part of Dave's story in the class it was all I could do to bring the class back together because people were crying and responding to the incredible story you are about to read. I have since had Dave share that story in church and became his translator as he shared it with Ani's primarily Indonesian speaking family.

The story you are about to read is one of survival, determination, and God's sovereignty. But maybe most important, it is a story of forgiveness. I've told Dave's story more than one time to churches, friends, and family members. I often conclude that story with statements like, "If Dave Pearman can forgive the wrongs done to him then anyone can." If Dave can turn out OK, so can any of us. I know it is never good to compare, and Dave's story isn't one for comparison but one for inspiration. Dave Pearman's story will inspire you to forgive, to survive life's hardest times, and to know that God has a plan.

—Jeff Hartensveld

Preface

I'm not a hero or a business magnate. I haven't accomplished great feats or valiantly led others to do great things. What I have done is overcome each and every storm in my life. I have not done it alone. The Supreme Creator lovingly watched over me and helped me climb over the obstacles one by one even before I knew Him. Really, I'm no different than any person in the world. My hopes are that by reading my story, you will find encouragement and courage to go over one more obstacle, one more hill, one more mountain until you find safety and life on the other side of the ridge. This is my journey I want to share with you.

My early childhood is filled with much mystery since I don't know exactly where I came from. I don't know anything about my birth parents. Did they not like me? Or did they give up on me for my benefit? I'd like to think it was the second one. Or maybe it was just my birth mother? Then what happened to her, and why was the father not around? Two months before I was born in South Korea, there was a political coup that caused a change in the government. Did my father die in some kind of battle, leaving my mom without any means to support me? Or were they even married at all? Was I an accident, a result of unwanted pregnancy? Was my mom raped and so I was also unwanted, even by her? I also noticed my jaw isn't like the typical Korean jaw that is so broad - maybe my father was not even a Korean? Did I have siblings or half-siblings? If yes, was I the only one given up? I had so many unanswered questions I didn't know where to turn for answers.

I could have gone on and on thinking about a thousand possibilities for my story, but after a while I just had to stop. In fact, I didn't like to think in that direction. I didn't want to start a self-pity spiral. This was built inside of me since I was young, probably a defense mechanism to cope with my past.

From what I remember, I never knew hunger nor homelessness. I'm forever grateful for this. I know other orphans had it harder - some had to live on the streets and beg for food. Some were in the wrong hands and were trained to be criminals or worse. *The Lord has always watched over me, even before I knew Him.*

Still, for the longest time, deep inside I wanted to reject this identity, a crippled Korean orphan whom nobody wanted because it was too painful, but as much as I tried to avoid my past, my mind had to make some sense of it. I always had wanted to forget my painful past - all of it, but from the urging of friends, the Lord gave me the bravery to go into my past. So when I was old enough to "go there," I gathered my information.

Over several weeks, I started recording on my phone what I could remember of my past. They weren't always coherent recollections, since sometimes I did them when I was lying in bed at night. Starting January of 2021 during the pandemic, I started forming my thoughts into more like a memoir - a list of factual short stories. After I finished the chronology, I had put down about 17,000 words, however, they still didn't have a life. I waited a whole year before my loving wife helped me out and did she ever!

Ani, my co-writer and wonderful wife, researched extensively from Korean history and culture, the adoption process, sentiments in South Korea and America during the early 1970s, and orphanages in South Korea. Once I inquired about my adoption records, it laid the timeline before my adoption. My adoption records showed that I was an orphan since birth. There was no record of my father, nor of my mother, nor any relatives. The record mentioned my date of birth and that I was from the family origin of Dan Yan. I was placed at City Baby Home in Seoul, South Korea. They called me Juhn Joong Ki, just a common boy's name. I stayed in City Baby Home from birth to around four years old. I had one vaccination for DPT two days before I was moved to Christian Adoption Program of Korea (CAPOK) Foster Care. From CAPOK, I was transferred from one foster home to another, then to Holt's Orphanage. After a short while, I was transferred to my first adopted home in Michigan, USA. Finally, due to unusual circumstances, I found my final place in the loving home of the Pearman family in Oregon.

As you read on, you may discover a little bit of yourself trying to cope with the life given to you.

(Note: Some names have been changed to protect their privacy.)

CHAPTER

01

The Early Years

The eyes of the Lord are in every place,
Watching the evil and the good.
Proverbs 15:3

She pushed the multi-colored plaid bag into my hand and shouted, "I'm sending you back to Korea!" It was a cold, dark October night. She had taken me to the first floor of the three-story house. There I stood, bawling my eyes out with only my plaid bag in my hand.

She was supposed to be my mother, though an adopted one. Being an orphan all my life, I didn't dare to wish for a mother who would love me unconditionally, care for all my needs, and protect me from vulnerability, fears, dangers, and threats. I didn't ask for any of those things.

Anyway, I was just a brand-new addition to this family. I had only been living with them for one month. I barely knew English, much less my place in this family. All I wanted was to be accepted in this new land of America and by my new family. I just wanted to be a good boy, to please them, and make it work.

She ignored my cries and as fast as she could, her hands unclothed me. I was ashamed. I was 10. I knew this was shameful, but I didn't dare make her angrier. She put three paint cans in front of me. She told me to get on top of the paint cans. Then she put two paint cans full of paint, one in each of my hands and told me to hold them straight out. I cried and cried and begged for her forgiveness. My arms were burning now from the weight of the paint cans. My scrawny legs felt like jelly – as if they would collapse at any second. My head was throbbing from sobbing so hard and so long. She didn't care. I thought of the other children upstairs. *Would they hear me cry and come to my rescue?*

She looked at me with fierceness in her face. I could tell she was not finished with me. She threw me outside. She also threw my plaid bag outside, my lone possession that I brought from Korea. I was still naked in the dark, cold, October night in Michigan. Ignoring the physical pain, all I could feel was the pain of rejection. The pain of confusion. The pain of shame, for being naked. I was 10 years old. I knew being naked did something to my dignity.

I wished I knew what I had done wrong. I wished I could just die there. I cried until I couldn't cry anymore.

At that moment of self-pity, I thought the only person who might come to my rescue was the dad. I never really had a chance to interact with him since he was always working, and I was left at home with the mom and the children, my siblings. But he was the dad; surely, he could make things better.

I thought of walking out to the end of the long, dirt driveway of their house. Maybe I should carry my little bag to the end of that road and put myself in that little bag. I imagined if I did, when the dad came home, he would see me in the bag and have pity on me. Maybe he would pick me up and talk to his wife so I would be accepted again into their home, into their family.

But I knew that wouldn't work. Here I was still outside, alone, naked, and miserable. My head hurt even more. My arms were cramping with pain. My legs felt weak and numb as I stood on the cold ground. I was shivering and shaking from the freezing breeze on my head and my whole body. There was no other house I could run to and seek help. There was no neighborhood. All houses were so far from each other. *Who could help me?*

Before, in Korea I was strong enough to survive. Now, I was living in a foreign land with a foreign language, trying to fit into a foreign family. I had almost run out of hope. My thoughts suddenly went to the time at Holt's orphanage in Korea, where they shared about Jesus. I never knew Him or asked Him into my life, but suddenly, out of total desperation I cried out loudly, "JESUS!"

1.1 The First Memories

"Joong Ki! Come to the table and eat!" Halmoni (Grandmother) called. I was playing with my one and only wooden top that had a stick to make it spin. I quickly stopped playing and went to the table. Halmoni was serving a bowl of steamed brown rice, vegetables, and kimchi. We were not rich enough to buy processed white rice. Once in a while there were fish and meat in the soup, and sometimes there would be fruit as a dessert.

We waited for Hal-abeoji (Grandfather) to join us at the table. Hal-abeoji was to be honored, obeyed, and respected. We wouldn't start eating if he didn't start first. We ate at a low table while sitting on the floor. I was around three or four years old and knew how to use a spoon. I loved kimchi over warm brown rice, and I always enjoyed the fresh lettuce texture in my mouth.

Suddenly I had the urge to relieve myself. Quickly, I went to the pot near the table, and peed just in time. Grandmother praised me, and I even got a little approving look from Grandfather. I was happy and proud of my achievement of mastering potty training skills. This memory would later be the first memory of my life.

After our meal, Grandmother cleaned me, then I went back to playing with my wooden top. She got up, cleaned up the dining area, and brought everything to the kitchen. Grandfather rested. I knew better than to bother him. Grandmother had told me that Grandfather was out and about since early in the morning every day, so I was to be quiet when he returned home. Grandmother was always busy around the house, but I could always find her if I needed help. This way the house was peaceful and in harmony.

We lived in a small house in the Kooro-dong area. The house was simple with several rooms. The dining area and the kitchen were connected, and then there was a big front room with windows. Even with windows, it was still dark. Then there was another room for sleeping. It also wasn't well lit. I played mostly in the dark.

Suddenly I heard my name being called, "Joong Ki, Myung-Sook is here. You both can play together."

Myung-Sook was an older girl around six years old who visited once in a while. She could have been another foster child, or a visiting grandchild, or a neighbor's child needing to be babysat from time to time. I didn't end up playing with Myung-Sook too much. She wanted to help Grandmother in the kitchen.

Grandmother was slender and beautiful. Her hair was gray and long. I imagined she must have been more beautiful when she was young with black hair. Now her eyes smiled when she smiled. She liked to touch my whole face when she talked to me. That made me feel loved, wanted, and secure. I didn't interact with Grandfather too much, but I didn't mind a bit. Grandmother was enough for me.

1.2 The First Joys

This is the day which the Lord has made;
Let us rejoice and be glad in it.
Psalm 118:24

About a week later, I went with Grandmother to visit her friends. She got permission from Grandfather to go out once in a while. The friends lived down by the river and did their daily clothes washing with the scrubbing boards. I was told to bow down politely and call them grandmothers and aunties.

"Joong Ki, you're so handsome. I'm going to keep you. You're going to come live with me!" one woman started teasing me.

I started crying, "No, No......!" and hugged and hid behind my grandma.

Grandmother laughed. "Stop teasing him!" she said to her friends. "Look, you have made Joong Ki afraid."

The women kept teasing me and taking my hands as if they would take me away from my family. "Don't worry! I won't leave you here," Grandmother said as she grabbed my arm.

I was not a talkative or outgoing child, and maybe a little clingy to my grandma. I didn't know they were just joking.

One of the ladies said, "Where did you get him again?"

Grandmother replied, "Oh, he was at Baby Home and then was taken to CAPOK Foster Care. Then he was assigned by CAPOK to Kooro-dong foster home to live with us. Shhh! Joong Ki believes we are his real grandparents. That's why we taught him to call us Halmoni and Hal-abeoji (grandmother and grandfather)."

They kept on chatting, and I stayed close to Grandmother.

It seems we visited a Korean temple once in a great while, but I hardly remember what went on there. The temple had a massive yard and ample rooms inside. The architecture showed it was likely a Buddhist temple - with intricate designs on the roofs, ceilings, doors, and railings. I admired the colors, as they were vibrant and lively in a way that made my heart merry. I enjoyed the peaceful and quiet vibes. I often stopped to take in the beauty of the temple. I had never seen something so gorgeous.

"Joong Ki! Walk fast and stay close to Halmoni," Grandmother said, worrying that I would get lost in the crowds of people. Grandfather walked fast; we both tried to follow him closely so we wouldn't lose him.

It was a celebration of Buddha's birthday. After some chanting and rituals, the temple served simple meals with vegetables to the visitors. It was a good time as a family.

Not long after that, Grandmother told me, "Joong Ki. You're a big boy now. It's time to go to school and learn with other kids. This is how you spell your name in Hangul 전중기 Juhn Jung Ki. You will need to write it on all your papers you turn in to the teacher." Hangul is the Korean alphabet.

I was so excited. Although I was a reserved child in terms of social interactions, I was a daring, independent, and adventurous child. I wanted to know how to read Hangul like Grandfather. I wanted to learn. Mostly, I wanted to play with other boys.

I enjoyed school, and learning was a fun way to meet my teachers and friends. I was independent. As soon as it was time for me to start school, I wasn't afraid to walk home from school by myself. I knew how to get to places like to the harbor. It soon became my favorite place to find solace. I loved seeing the blueness of the sky meeting the blueness of the water. I loved all the vastness of the sky and the ocean.

One particular day, my school friends told me that the United States Air Force was going to give an airplane show at the bay. Just like all the people in my school and family, I was fond of the United States Military. After leaving my school gear at home, I ran as fast as I could to the bay. The bay was a steep harbor surrounded on one side by a rocky hill. It was from those hills that people could crowd and see the airplane drills. I was on one side of the rocky hill, waiting with such excitement. The hills made a u-shaped bay, and on the other two sides of the u-shape were housing areas. At one point, the airplanes were dropping bombs onto old naval ships. What an amazing sight that was! I was thrilled even more at the end when a bomb was dropped a little too close to the housing areas and exploded with a large boom. The crowds cheered, and I shouted at the top of my lungs.

The airshow made a huge impression on me and gave me fondness for something related to the United States. Secretly, I imagined that maybe I too could ride in a jet airplane someday. Little did I know that the Lord put a seed

25

of faith and vision inside of me that day, and that in the near future He would ordain my steps to come to the United States on a jet airplane.

The dream to ride in an airplane didn't come too soon, but what came next would change my course and outlook on life forever.

1.3 The First Tears

The eyes of the Lord are toward the righteous
And His ears are open to their cry.
Psalm 34: 15

Koreans have this ability to sense what people are thinking and feeling. They can even gauge the room and situation in order to create connection, trust, and harmony. It is called "nunchi" which literally means "eye-measure." They teach their children from a young age to read between the lines of the unwritten and unspoken clues. Nunchi is like a combination of emotional intelligence and situational awareness, but with speed. Thoughts and feelings are fluid and can change at any time depending on the situation, so nunchi is always "on". Koreans can read people and situations fluidly as they are happening. Something could be pleasant to start with, but then could turn for the worse. Koreans would know how to respond in harmony with the situation when it was pleasant and when it was not, because they followed their nunchi. In English, it's called discernment or a sixth sense.

Grandfather was talking with Grandmother when I came home from school that day. They were suddenly quiet and acting weird. My nunchi said something was up. I knew it must be something important and serious. Maybe it was about Grandfather's work or the relatives. I proceeded as usual - eating, practicing my Hangul, and playing with my paper airplane - while making sure I didn't add extra problems to the household.

One January morning in 1968, Grandmother told me we were going to the doctor for a regular health check-up. It was freezing, but we still had to go. This was unusual, my nunchi said, because Grandmother didn't like going out when it was too cold. Her weak knees would rattle when the weather was freezing.

But the visit was important, she told Grandfather. So we went. When we got to the doctor's office, the main doctor went through a full health check-up of me and asked my grandmother questions I didn't understand. Then he said he was happy that I was in good health and proceeded to give me the DPT immunization shot. I was getting familiar with immunization shots –

Grandmother kept my records inside her purse. That was my third DPT shot already, and afterward we returned home from the doctor's office.

Months went by very quickly. Suddenly it was summer and the weather was very warm. I was playing near Grandmother when she suddenly called my name, "Joong Ki!" Then her voice became sober.

My nunchi went up again and I asked, "Is there something wrong?" The way she called me was different than any other time.

I went to her immediately.

Grandmother's voice cracked as she told me, "Joong Ki, listen to Halmoni, okay? You are going to be moving to a different house and living with another family."

"What do you mean going to a different family?" I exclaimed.

There was no answer.

"Halmoni, what do you mean? Why can't I stay here with you and Hal-abeoji? You are my grandparents!"

"Joong Ki, listen to Halmoni. Halmoni and Hal-abeoji are not your real grandparents. Halmoni and Hal-abeoji are *like* your grandparents. We have loved taking care of you, but now we are too old. You have to move to a different family who is younger and has children for you to play with," Halmoni said, but I couldn't hear all the words, because I was crying.

My world was shattered right then and there.

My grandparents were the only family I could recollect. I believed in my mind and with all of my heart Halmoni and Hal-abeoji were my grandparents, my *real* family. I didn't know otherwise. I didn't remember having any mom, dad, brother, or sister. I tried to ask before but Grandmother didn't answer, so I thought I should never ask again. As I said, the older girl, Myung-Sook, came to Grandmother's house once in a while, but it was clear I didn't have any family connection to her. It seemed Myung-Sook had been coming more often. *Was I being replaced by her? Was she the real grandchild then?*

Confusion crowded my thoughts. *So, all this time, who were they to me, if not my grandparents?* Being that young, it was impossible for me to understand the concept of foster grandparents.

Or maybe it was my fault. I didn't obey them sometimes.

"Halmoni, did I do something wrong? I am so sorry."

Grandmother put her hands on my whole face, her usual way to comfort me, but this time it wasn't comforting at all. I shed more tears.

"Joong Ki, you're a good boy. Halmoni tells you all the time," she said, quietly. Then she looked at Grandfather.

Grandfather tried to explain, "Halmoni and Hal-abeoji are getting too old to take care of you, so you need to stay with another family."

"Please let me stay with you! You know I can take care of myself! I am always independent!" I pleaded over and over.

But Grandfather shook his head. It was decided.

I was dreading the day I would be moved to another foster home. The people whom I called grandparents didn't want me anymore. My sense of love and belonging, security and protection, a home, and a family, were taken away just like that. My heart was broken to pieces. I especially loved my Halmoni, my grandmother.

"Will I see you again, Halmoni?" I cried, as she got me ready.

"Yes, maybe… Yes." Grandmother answered, but my nunchi somehow told me that it would be the last time I saw her.

CHAPTER

02

A Tough Boy

The Lord is in His holy temple; the Lord's throne is in heaven; His eyes behold, His eyelids test the sons of men.
Psalm 11:4

2.1 A Vow

You have taken account of my wanderings; Put my tears in Your
bottle. Are they not in Your book?
Psalm 56:8

Once I was transported to the house on top of the hill, my mixed feelings of confusion, fears, hurt, rejection, and brokenness exploded into tearful crying. In fact, I bawled all day. I cried long rivers of tears that were felt all the way down to my gut muscles, as I sat on the front step of that wooden shack. The shack was the second house I would live in.

Into the pool of tears below me, I vowed, *I will never be hurt like this again!* That declaration would mark me for a very long time. That declaration made me a tough little boy, then later a tough man. In the months that followed, I obediently walked to school every day and tried to make the best of a bad situation. I vowed I would not let anything defeat me. I was back to my normal self, except for the hurt deep inside my soul that no one else could see.

I was trying to be tough with my own strength. This defense mechanism became my winning formula. I would not allow anything to make me sad. I would be tough for any bad situation. If I couldn't defend myself, who would? Nobody so far wanted to fight for me.

I didn't become a bad boy, but later I struggled to feel compassion for other people. If I could survive without other people's compassion, I thought others should also be tough and strong like I was. The last thing I wanted was anyone's pity. I made sure I was smart, independent, and not causing any trouble. In fact, I would become a problem solver, to make sure I wasn't a burden to anyone nor seen as a weak person. Little did I know, I was trying to protect myself from being hurt by others again, from rejection, abandonment, or being despised.

After that day, it was hard for me to cry again. My tears were used up on the day I was moved from the first foster home to the second.

I didn't know that God was watching, but He was. And He did so much more than just watch. He collected my tears in the bottle, recorded each one in His book, and continued to work all things for my good.

2.2 Starting Again

For I will set My eyes on them for good, and I will bring them
again to this land; and I will build them up and not overthrow
them, and I will plant them and not pluck them up.
Jeremiah 24:6

My second foster family lived in Sangdo-dong. The family was very nice and wanted to take care of me. My documents from CAPOK, the foster home organization, had stated that the first foster family at Kooro-dong had some problems, and somehow this second family was willing to accommodate me. They also got reports of my behavior, school reports, and health documents.

When I got there, it was July. According to my report, I just turned 7 years old. I remember it was a hot and wet summer because summer had monsoon months.

"Joong Ki, we are your family now. Please tell us what you need," the mom said again. Maybe she wanted to comfort me for crying so much on my first day.

I think they all tried to welcome me and make me feel like a family. Sadly, I didn't pay attention to how much they were trying to love me, because I was busy guarding my heart from being hurt again. I just stayed quiet but I nodded to be polite. My heart was still heavy from sadness.

The mom quickly showed me around the house. The house was just a shack consisting of a few rooms. The shack was built on a small plot of farmland on top of a hill. Since the house didn't have a modern toilet, the family had another small shack to do our routine "business". The manure from this shack would be used to fertilize the farmland.

Deep inside, I was grateful a family wanted to take me in. I knew they probably had to sacrifice something to accommodate me. I would repay their kindness by being responsible, well-behaved, and not causing any trouble.

"Joong Ki, let's get ready. We need to take you to the clinic for an injection," the mom said. It was the fourth day after I arrived. The mom and the dad took me to the city clinic so I could get the first dose of the polio vaccine. I was expecting a painful injection like last time, but it turned out to

33

be something they put in my mouth. It was the first dose of the oral poliovirus vaccine (OPV). The doctor told my new foster parents I was still not out of the woods yet with the polio virus, since the vaccine worked most effectively after three doses.

The gorgeous view from my new home distracted me from dwelling on my grandparents and the life I had lost. Since the shack was built on the hilltop, I was spoiled with such a panoramic view of Seoul in an acre plot field. It was like a vast canvas that changed colors from sunrise to sundown. It made me happy, relaxed, and peaceful. Sometimes on a rainy day, I could see a rainbow on the other side of a half sunny day. We had a special name when that happened. We called it Tiger Day.

As a grade-schooler I marveled at such amazing sights, especially during a cold yet warm, rainy yet sunny winter day. I guess that was how God comforted me, although I didn't know Him yet.

2.3 Stricken by Polio

Pity me, pity me,
O you my friends,
For the hand of God has struck me.
Job 19: 21

As I was trying to be strong and brave in my own strength, I didn't know I was going to face another calamity in my young life. At this time, I was in the second grade.

One day, I became very ill and missed school for weeks. I had hardly been ill before that. I was small and thin to the point of being scrawny, but I was always healthy and strong, with a keen mind and a full tank of energy to run around and be resourceful.

Yet that day started with a sore throat and nausea. The mom told me to stay at home and skip school. I didn't have the energy to get up anyway. Then I started having a fever and extreme headache, followed by strange stomach pains.

"Oh Joong Ki, you're burning up. Take this medicine," the mom said. She gave me some medicine, but after a few days, I still didn't get better. I wanted to be strong and not cause trouble, but I couldn't stand it anymore.

"Mom, my body and leg hurt all over. Especially my leg - it feels like something is stabbing it." I tried hard not to cry.

The mom told the dad, and they took me to the hospital.

Their facial expressions told me it wasn't good.

"I am so sorry to inform you that Joong Ki is infected with polio. It's been confirmed the virus is in his stool specimen," the doctor said to the parents. "When he started feeling the pains in that leg, that means he was already having paresthesia. The virus has moved from his gut to affect the central nervous system. When I checked his reflexes on the left leg, they weren't responding. This means the muscles there aren't responding. The conclusion is, Joong Ki has shown the onset of paralysis of the left leg. Fortunately, he already took one dose of the OPV, so the damage is not as bad as it could have been. Both of his arms are fine, and the right leg seems to be spared. Polio will not affect his cognitive abilities, but, yes, unfortunately, his muscles will wither on the left leg and the bones will not grow. So, as he grows taller, he will be limping from not having the muscles to support his walk and the difference in length of the two legs. At this point, he will need rehabilitation to learn to walk again as soon as he recovers from the disease." The doctor added sternly, "I think you need to do something about the outhouse, or there might be other victims."

I ended up missing school for weeks. I don't remember much actually. The only thing I remember from that time was that all my classmates visited me at the hospital. My foster parents didn't say anything. The doctor and nurses didn't say anything, but my nunchi said if I needed to be hospitalized, then the illness must be quite serious. I also thought it was odd that my classmates visited me, because it wasn't like I was a popular child. Why did they make a fuss to visit me? How long was I in the hospital? I didn't know what had happened to me.

I was told later that I had contracted polio most likely from that outhouse. The casualty from this battle with polio was my left leg. The nerves had stopped working in some parts and atrophied certain muscles in my leg. I could no longer lift my leg from sitting position. I couldn't lift my toes on that leg. I could no longer run or even walk normally. I had to "throw" my left leg with the hip muscle when I walked.

2.4 My Winning Formula

They also gave me gall for my food
And for my thirst they gave me vinegar to drink.
Psalm 69: 21

I was told to be grateful. Apparently, I had the first polio vaccine, but it needed to be done three times before it would really work. Still, it saved me from what could have been worse. Although it was hard to be grateful, I was. They said over and over that polio was rampant in the 1950s, a decade before I was born. It quickly became one of the most serious communicable diseases with dire consequences such as death. In some cases, patients who became paralyzed were kept alive in iron lung machines. It could hit anyone, rich or poor, even the President of the United States, Franklin D. Roosevelt (1882-1945), at the age of 39. I knew I could have been worse after seeing the pictures of people with worse conditions than mine.

I was grateful, but I resented the fact that it happened to me. I didn't know how to navigate that feeling.

Every day I watched that awful disease destroy the nerve cells of my left leg from the inside. My muscles could no longer receive signals from my brain or my spinal cord. Not having the nerve stimulation, my left leg suffered muscle atrophy, weakness, poor control, and finally complete paralysis.

Still, I was stubborn and committed to fight this polio. I told myself I would be okay. After months of rehabilitation, I was able to walk, although now with a very noticeable limp. I dared not run. My left leg was now noticeably shorter and weaker, but my fighting spirit was steadfast. I sent a message to myself loud and clear: *I will not let anything hurt me again.* This tough stance, my new winning formula, my defense mechanism, seemed to work. It made me not worry too much about my condition.

Yet I grieved quietly in my heart for the loss of my good left leg, although from the outside I never allowed myself to break down in tears again. Deep inside I was saddened mostly because I loved sports, and I thought I would be good at them.

The family took me to rehabilitation faithfully. After months of rehabilitation, I went to school like any other child. When others had physical sports time, I remained in the classroom. Sometimes I wished that I could run around and do sports with them, but instead I just watched them through the windows as they played on the field below me. Sometimes I would be very curious and look into other people's bags to waste some time, but I knew better than to take anything that wasn't mine. I quickly occupied myself with something else.

After some time, the sadness left me. Then all I felt was numbness. I was numb about having polio. I was numb about not seeing the old couple that I thought were my grandparents. They slowly faded away from my memories. I was so used to having pains or trials in my life that I didn't even let them get to me. I didn't allow myself to be sad or make room to be disappointed, but I just kept pressing those feelings down.

My foster mom felt a bit guilty that I contracted polio at her house. She made sure I had all my vaccinations needed: vaccines for DPT, cholera, typhoid, and especially the remaining two polio vaccines.

"Joong Ki, there is a healing service being held, and I want to take you there," she said. She sounded excited.

"What is it?" I had never heard of such a thing.

"Well, God in heaven is big and powerful. He heals people from all kinds of sicknesses. I want to take you there so people can pray for you and your polio leg can become strong and normal again," she answered.

The healing service was held outside on a huge field with a covered stage for the speakers. My foster mom went out of her way to take me near the covered stage. I believe it was a Christian healing service. This was my first encounter with the Christian faith, in a way. My foster mom really believed God would heal my leg. We sat on the ground midway to the right of the stage. I could barely see the people on stage. I don't remember what the man said, but my foster mom prayed and prayed for my leg to be healed. At the encouragement of my foster mom, I confessed with my mouth that I would be healed. I also had to repeat the confession of the leader up front. I dreamed a little of how amazing it would be if I was healed. I don't know if I didn't have enough faith or what, but after the evening of this service, my left leg did not change.

I wasn't disappointed because I had protected myself from having hopes, and when you don't have hopes, you don't get disappointed. But I think my foster mom was disappointed. Seeing her being so saddened that I didn't receive my miracle made me realize that she sincerely desired for me to be healed. I didn't learn to know God from that healing service. Strangely, I didn't even feel that He wasn't being fair to me. I didn't complain or get mad at God, and I didn't entertain self-pity.

I just focused on being smart, strong, independent, and a problem solver. This combination would be my winning formula. And with my winning formula, I would take care of myself no matter what.

2.5 Being Uprooted to the Orphanage

Make me to hear joy and gladness,
Let the bones which You have broken rejoice.
Psalm 51: 8

One good thing about having polio was that the family really heeded the doctor's warning about the outhouse. Soon we moved to a normal house in a crowded neighborhood below the hilltop. This house was definitely a big upgrade from a shack since it was more secure. However, it was not securely built. When it stormed during the monsoon season, we had waterfalls coming down from the ceiling. We ran and retrieved as many pots and pans as we could to catch the rain and spare the floor.

When I started living in a normal house, my friends and I would visit several neighborhood dojangs (training sites) where we saw many amazing feats of martial arts students. We saw them climb walls and run along the walls with ease. I admired their agility. They also showed amazing acrobatic flips and kicks. I could only dream that someday I could do such wonderful feats, but I knew it was only a dream. So, I shut my feelings down to protect myself from being disappointed or having self-pity.

I was afraid to love this second family. I started to feel guilty because I intentionally didn't allow myself to invest many feelings toward them. I expressed my gratitude to them for taking care of me, but deep inside I knew the outhouse caused polio to come into my life. I didn't know how to deal with that. It was like being grateful and ungrateful. How could I process that? So, it was better not to think about it at all. Also, why bother investing so much love if someday they would uproot me, or I would be uprooted from them again?

Slowly, I started feeling more comfortable in this second family. Maybe they could become my family forever. Maybe I should open my heart to them. As I was beginning to open my heart to this family, God had another plan. One day, my foster mom took me to a high-rise office building in the center of Seoul. There were a dozen or so other kids. I had no idea why I was there.

My nunchi said it was for an important visit, but I wasn't comfortable with what kind of place this could be.

It was at that moment that I noticed a boy moving on the floor. He was crawling in a peculiar sliding motion with his hands scooting on the floor to get around. *What happened to him? Did he have polio too?* I tried to avoid and ignore him. I think the sight of him being disabled made me uncomfortable. What if people group us together as "the crippled boys"? I felt bad. I wanted to feel compassion for him, but I felt it would backfire on me since people would feel compassion (or pity) for him and then for me too. I definitely didn't want that to happen. So, I just ignored him, although I couldn't stop thinking of him.

In a short while, maybe less than a month, I was told I would be moved to an orphanage. I was tough now, so it didn't matter to me one way or another. I had made room in my heart for the possibility of being uprooted again from the current family, so in a way I already expected this.

Maybe my second foster mom took me to that high rise office to register me for the orphanage. I didn't ask. I didn't want to know. My winning formula said to be tough and just go with the flow.

So that ended my time with the second family. I was there for only 20 months. I didn't even cry when I left them. I was transferred to the Holt Orphanage at Ilsan Center, Seoul, South Korea. There were some other kids crying in the minibus taking us there, but I had no more sentimental tears left in my life. I reminded myself I would be tough, however, I felt bad not crying with them. I pretended I was crying too, so others wouldn't feel bad, but that same strange numb feeling returned deep inside me.

CHAPTER

03

Life at Holt Ilsan Orphanage

Turn to me and be gracious to me,
For I am lonely and afflicted.
Psalm 25: 16

3.1 The Orphan Stigma

For my father and my mother have forsaken me,
But the Lord will take me up.
Psalm 27:10

Before I share about the Holt Orphanage, please allow me to explain Korean culture. This was the background of my life growing up, but it is still true even in this modern age. Korean society prides itself in the long records of family lines. One's ancestry and bloodline are very important and can be traced back for hundreds of years. They make up one's identity. Maintaining a high honor of reputation and family name is what children should do for their parents and ancestors. Thus, when a single, unwed woman becomes pregnant, she knows she has failed her parents and her ancestors.

The cause of the pregnancy doesn't matter. Whether it is her fault or not, she will be frowned upon. There is no redemption for her. She will carry a stigma and will be under prejudices forever. Her parents, and even friends, will be embarrassed and will not want to be part of her struggles in pregnancy, giving birth, and raising the child. In order to maintain the family reputation and save face, the pregnant woman will have to fight alone. The best thing to do is hide her pregnancy from the parents and friends and give birth in a secret place.

The Korean welfare system for the single, unwed mothers requires them to put their illegitimate babies on the family registry. These poor mothers then have documents readily accessible to any and all potential employers. This system makes it hard for these poor women to find a job and a spouse someday. The stigma is so strong, it is as if they were immoral women. They would rather keep themselves anonymous for this reason. They would find a way to give birth and abandon the babies somewhere.

Therefore, orphans have this stigma too. They are the lowest caste of Korean society. An orphan is treated as a "nonperson", and "identity-less." Orphans in South Korean orphanages are rarely adopted by Korean families. Most stay until they turn 18 years old and become adults. From then on, they must live on their own.

As for me, I never really felt this stigma, maybe because I was placed by CAPOK into two caring foster families. From my earliest memories, all I knew were foster homes. My foster family was my family, since they were the only family I had. They took care of me the best they could, and I did my best to be a good boy. I never questioned each family's sincerity in taking me in, and I didn't question being transferred to the orphanage. I never wanted to be a troublemaker. I never felt I was that different than any other kids at school whether it was with the foster families or at the orphanage.

The reason why adoption is so rare in South Korea is because most orphans come with little or no information. Potential adoptive parents are afraid of the unknowns, such as prenatal care (what if the pregnancy was not healthy?) and any parental history (what if the birth mother or father has some kind of mental or psychological problems?). Couples who struggle with infertility are also frowned upon. They are stigmatized to the point that couples who want to adopt would fake a pregnancy in front of parents, friends, and colleagues, and then arrange for the baby secretly.

Even if a couple has the courage to adopt a baby from a Korean orphanage, it is more likely for them to adopt a perfectly healthy baby. I couldn't help but wonder, *Is there even a family for me, an orphan with no ancestry and bloodline to trace, AND crippled?*

3.2 An Answer to God's Call

Your eyes have seen my unformed substance;
And in Your book were all written
The days that were ordained for me,
When as yet there was not one of them.
Psalm 139: 16

In 1950, Dr. Bob Pierce, the President of World Vision, spoke at a meeting in Eugene, Oregon to bring awareness about a particularly dark aspect of the Korean War: the "GI babies" left behind by the military men. These mixed-race babies of American fathers and Korean mothers were abandoned or left to die in the army dump, garbage dump, and any secret, hidden places. Or their ashamed mothers would hide them until they couldn't hide them anymore, then these blond haired, blue-eyed Korean children or Black-Korean children would be left wandering on the streets and receiving abuse from other children and adults. Dr. Pierce was showing film after film of the plight of hundreds of illegitimate children needing rescuing and what his organization's missionary efforts had done to help. Sharing how the Koreans were very race conscious and would never accept mixed-race children into their society, he asked for partnerships with the audience to sponsor an orphan at $10 per month.

Harry and Bertha started sending $10 each month in response to the orphan plea, but deep inside they knew God wanted them to do more. They could never forget the hundreds of children that represented so much suffering. They were poorly nourished, weak, and needed God's love and protection. Then they found out there were other children who were forsaken. Their parents had been killed during the war or died from a disease. These were children who were crippled, blind, or in poor health and didn't have a place in their own families. Would they answer the call of God to do something with these kids to make a difference in their lives?

In 1955, Harry and Bertha adopted eight children, four boys and four girls ranging from babies to three and a half years-old from South Korea. In 1956, they founded the Holt International Children's Services to place unwanted South Korean babies and children with potential adoptive parents from the States. What was more significant, the Holt orphanage had the heart to take care of those children who were disabled or had special needs who would not be cared for anywhere else.

They rescued the most undesirable, stigmatized, and socially rejected orphans so they would have a place to stay, education, and more importantly, a new identity. They inspired many American couples to sponsor or adopt these precious children so they too would have a future and hope. The South Korean government really supported them. Once these children were adopted, birth mothers became legally non-existent in the system, a legal erasure of these "socially unacceptable women".

Why was this significant to me, personally? By the standard of Korean society, I was among the lowest caste of orphans. I was an orphan with polio. I would not have been accepted in the Korean orphanage. I would never be adopted because of my disability, but I didn't know this. I was a young and vulnerable orphan who couldn't decide for myself; my childhood was one transition after another. I was just "flowing with the system".

But the Good Lord had really been watching over me. He didn't just move me from one place to another, He made sure my steps were numbered and He did have a plan for me, even in my suffering. By allowing me to have polio, He was actually making a way for me to be placed in a special orphanage. The Holt Orphanage would later be my ticket to being adopted in America.

The Good Lord laid out every moment of my life before a single day had dawned. He knew how to turn bad things into good. He navigated even the ill decisions and circumstances of people to bring about His goodness. He knew how to make all things, good and bad, work together for my good. He knew I would learn all these nuggets of truths about His character later in my life.

3.3 A Busy Start at Holt Orphanage

You have turned for me my mourning into dancing;
You have loosed my sackcloth and girded me with gladness.
Psalm 30:11

The Holt Orphanage was very good at record keeping. I arrived on March 5th, 1970, and right away my documentation started. Dr. Mulder, an American doctor, looked at my previous records. These included my administration information, social information, physical appearance description, developmental evaluation, reason of referral, medical history, vaccination records, tests (chest x-ray and TB skin test), and weight. Then he made a referral report to Holt which was translated by Kim. C. H. At that point, I was number 7253 at Holt, after being number 122 in CAPOK.

Early months were busy months for Holt to start my rigorous documentation - not only for me to be part of the Holt Orphanage, but more importantly, to be part of the Holt Adoption Program. Little did I know that they were already planning for me to be adopted by a family in America. Not every child going through their organization would be adopted; some would stay at the orphanage in Korea until they became independent adults. They'd never leave the country, but the Holt leadership determined it would be better for my future to be adopted by a family in the US. All along, the Lord had assigned adoption for my future, and was using the Holt agency to fulfill this part of my life.

They worked fast. In order to be adopted by a family in the States, I would need to have:

1. a valid passport
2. several current photos
3. adoption certificate for immigration
4. a certificate of orphanhood
5. a copy of the Korean Family Registration (Ho Juk Deung Bon) registered at the Court of Home Affairs of Seoul and signed by the chief officer of the district office
6. a thorough medical examination report to apply for a visa at the American Consul

7. Medical history reports
8. MHR that included my medical history, development in the area of education, my personality, habits, capabilities, and my emotional and mental health. All of this, so that I could be recommended for adoption.

Two weeks into my stay, they put me through a thorough medical examination to apply for the visa. The American Consul required the complete physical report, blood serological report, chest X-ray report, and anything else necessary. A few days later, they stamped PASSED on my first "visa physical". I would need to take this same kind of medical test for the visa application in August of the same year. I also passed the Medical History Report. Mr. Lim, B.W. created the report and recommended me for adoption.

Holt also assigned Mr. Kwan Soo Kim to be my guardian to process my application for certificate of appointment to the guardian. This was necessary so I would be formally considered a minor orphan in the orphanage, and therefore eligible for the adoption.

The first thing Mr. Kwan Soo Kim did for me as a guardian was to apply for my certificate of orphanhood. The application was certified by the chief officer of Ma Po District Office, Seoul (the same office that issued my guardianship). This certificate of orphanhood was an important step to begin the adoption process.

Later, Mr. Kwan Soo Kim made a statement of guardianship to transfer all his legal rights as my guardian. This enabled the Holt Adoption Program to consent to my medical and surgical treatments, to place me in an adoptive home, and to consent to my adoption.

I had another thorough physical examination for the visa process, and then in November of 1971 they started Child Progress Report No.1. This progress report needed to be repeated every few months to make sure I was truly a good candidate for adoption physically, mentally, emotionally, and socially, as long as the family was willing to accept my handicap. During these months, Holt also made sure I kept up with all my vaccinations.

Looking back, I am grateful for all the people who completed these meticulous processes in order to get my documentation ready. I was not aware of this, but the Lord provided all of them to be my helpers, my angels in human form.

3.4 Happy Days

You have turned my mourning into joyful dancing.
You have taken away my clothes of mourning and clothed me
with joy.
Psalm 30:11 NLT

"안녕하세요 [an nyeong ha seyo] I'm Seong-ho. What's your name?" A friendly boy slightly bowed his head and greeted me. "House mom said that you're new, and I am supposed to show you around," he said.

"안녕하세요 [an nyeong ha seyo], I'm Joong Ki. Thank you," I said, bowing slightly too.

Seong-ho started showing me the orphanage. We passed the dining room where boys were eating breakfast. They were eating brown rice, kimchi, and some fresh veggies. Seong-ho told them I was a new boy. As we walked, Seong-ho told me the rules of the house. Then we went to our cabin. There were 20 boys from ages six to 13 in one room. Seong-ho showed me the floor mat, which was to be unrolled for sleeping and rolled back up in the morning. He said they all feared the house mom. If they didn't obey—for example, if they didn't clean up their mess or make their belongings neat and organized—they would get a swat on their palms with a short, thick broom handle. I decided to obey right away.

My life at the Holt Orphanage was fun. Right away, I had many friends from my cabin. They became my brothers. The physical effects of polio did not slow me down as a child. I have many memories of playing all sorts of games with my friends. We enjoyed playing marbles. The game was simple, but fun. On a dirt floor, we made a square path. In each corner, we dug out a little circle. Then we'd take turns flicking our marbles to the hole. If we could get a marble into the first hole then we earned our right to go again for the second hole clockwise, and so on. It was almost like baseball. I remember the marbles being really pretty. We loved collecting them. Another marble game we enjoyed was played by shooting from outside a dirt circle, aiming to knock the marbles in the center outside to the circle. If we were able to knock them out, then the marbles belonged to us. After a while, I was quite good at the marble games. When I won marbles, I shouted with victory. I found out I was competitive in nature.

Another fun activity was battling beetles. My friends and I looked for good, strong, big beetles to fight. The best ones would have strong pinching power. We cheered for our own beetles as they battled with one another. It was very exciting. If our beetle died, we got another one from the tree.

We also played this fun slaps-match game with paper. I heard that this traditional game was as old as the Joseon Dynasty (1392-1897). This is how we played it. First, we got two colorful sheets of paper (we usually decorated them ourselves since colored paper was expensive). Then, we folded them together in such a way that it became a flat shaped card that was quite thick. They are called **ttakji** (딱지). Then, each player would put one ttakji on the ground. The others would try to hit the ttakji until it flipped over and went out of the line. If a player knocked the ttakji out, it became theirs. The object of the game was to get as many as ttakji on the ground as possible. This game was addictive. Again, my competitive side would show.

We made Korean style paper trick airplanes that flew back to you, much like a boomerang. It was certainly a fun trick to learn. We also learned Korean-style origami. I learned to make many things and still remembered how to fold small airplanes, boats, balls, and booming poppers.

Of course, on the top of my list of favorite games was the spinning top game, but this time, I learned to make the top from my friends. We'd make a spinning top by cutting one end of a small cylindrical piece of wood into a point. Then we would wind up a thick string around the wooden top with nail posts from top to bottom to make it continue spinning. The winner was the one who could spin the top the longest or knock the other's top off. I was good at this because I had played it all my life.

We never ran out of energy. We enjoyed sliding on cardboard sleds down the grassy hill right behind our cabin. We were resourceful at making our own toys. We made metal wheel toys from the ends of large cardboard freight cylinders and a metal coat hanger that we bent to make a hook to secure and push the wheel along.

I was so happy. I thought of this often: *Even if I don't get adopted, I am happy and content.* I had a band of brothers who became my family. We did everything together, from playing games I mentioned earlier, to taking a group bath; from watching American air force movies on the TV in the older kids' cabin, to planting watermelon seeds, and from frying white pieces of bread on top of an outdoor fire (this was special because bread was rare), to sizzling some tasty zucchinis on top of our metal fireplace in the middle of our cabin during cold winter months. And of course, studying with them too since education was important.

My sinful side showed itself also, although I wasn't aware. Every day we would walk to school together, which seemed like 30 minutes away. One path led through the small hillside and became muddy during the rainy season. The other path went through the morning outdoor market. One time, my friends dared me to steal a whole dried octopus jerky and I did. When we got to school, we had a bag inspection that day. I didn't know Jesus, but I hoped very hard that the teacher would not check my bag. He never did, so I got away with it. Still, I didn't repent.

The orphanage made sure we heard about Jesus. We would regularly go to Sunday school to learn about Jesus. I never really paid attention, but still, the seeds were planted in the soil of our hearts. We learned to read the Bible, and the teacher commented that I did well.

3.5 Leg Surgery

Look at the birds of the air, that they do not sow, nor reap nor gather into barns, and yet your heavenly Father feeds them. Are you not worth much more than they?
Matthew 6:26

Molly Holt was the daughter of founders Harry and Bertha Holt. She was a registered nurse (RN) and was the kindest soul. She was called either Molly or Unnie (언니), older sister, by the girls, and Noona (누나), older sisters, by us boys. I could really see that she was genuinely loving to me and to everyone.

One morning in December, Noona called me and said, "I have good news for you, Joong Ki. You're going to walk better." She smiled. I looked at her with a perplexed expression. Noona told me to sit down, and then she touched my left foot. "Look, I have arranged for you to have surgery on your left foot to straighten it out. Once this is straighter, Joong Ki, you'll walk so much better."

On December 7, 1970, a guardian took me by train to Wonju Union Christian Hospital in Kangwon Do, where I would have the surgery. Oh what a fun trip it was going to the city. I loved all the roads, bridges, and tall overpasses going up and down and intertwining with one another.

Prior to my surgery, the doctors checked my temperature, weight, height, skin complexion, vision, bones, and teeth. They performed a chest X-ray, and other tests to determine blood counts, as well as urinalysis and stool analysis. The results came back satisfactory for me to have the surgery.

On December 9th, I went under general anesthesia. The surgeon used a tourniquet technique to correct the left foot drop caused by polio. This hospital was affiliated with the Methodist Church in the USA and Canada, so I had an American doctor named Robert F. Roth, MD who oversaw the whole surgery. He later wrote the details of the surgery, the post-surgery care instructions, and the physical therapies I would need. I stayed in the hospital for 12 days to recover fully. At the time of surgery, a cast was put on my foot, and it was to stay for at least three and a half weeks. This would ensure all sutures stayed in place until they were ready to be removed so I could start physical therapy. The hospital gave a discount, so Holt only needed to pay a portion of the bill. I would need to return for a follow-up visit with Dr. Roth.

I remember distinctly that my surgery happened during the Christmas season, not because I was aware of the calendar, but because I received one or two presents during my stay in the hospital. (I loved the presents, but for some reason I didn't believe in Santa Claus.)

I remember a foreign, white, middle-aged couple with blond hair who visited me at my hospital room and gave me a gift. Of course, I was excited for the gift! Two vivid memories after the surgery were: that my left foot was sewn up with 21 stitches, and I got a wheelchair.

During recovery, it didn't take long to get back to my energetic self. I raced down the corridors in my wheelchair speedster every chance I got. The wheelchair and the racing gave me a good feeling about having the surgery.

When I got back to Holt's Orphanage, I still had to be in a wheelchair. I used it for a while and was getting really good at "driving" it everywhere.

Noona said it was time for me to graduate to the next step, which was using crutches. This was a long process that took many months to learn to walk again. I was not that patient, but Noona worked with me to rehabilitate my leg until I could use it again. I was so grateful for her. She was so kind and sweet that I wanted to train with her. She encouraged me to walk through the ramped pathway using the parallel bars on each side of my body. She was very patient with me. She was an angel of God for me.

During that time, while still navigating around on my crutches, I continued to play with my friends. My winning formula of being smart, strong, and independent came out again. I wanted to be as perfect as possible, without a sign of any weakness.

I soon proved myself wrong.

One time, my friend Seong-ho and I headed out of our cabin. After a short 5-to-10-minute walk, I felt my stomach cramping up. Oh no, I had to get to the bathroom quickly on my crutches. I tried to run as fast as I could, but since I was still navigating with my crutches, I didn't make it back in time to my cabin. I soiled all over my legs and my shorts. I was miserable, dirty, and ashamed. Soon I stank really badly. I was so touched that Seong-ho didn't run away from me. I cleaned up as best I could with the scratch writing papers as toilet paper. Seong-ho gave me some of his writing papers too.

"Do you want me to get you some clean clothes?" he asked.

I nodded. I was so glad he offered because I didn't know what to do.

"Please don't tell the house mom," I told him. My voice was so low that he almost couldn't hear me, but he nodded. We both knew the "stick punishment" the house mom gave to boys who soiled their pants. That night I regretted that the crutches made me walk slowly and caused my accident. At the same time, I was grateful to learn that my friend was very loyal and kind not to abandon me in my worst situation. He never told a soul. I didn't get the stick, and my other friends never knew.

I also realized that my winning formula to be smart, strong, and a problem solver might not always work, no matter how hard I tried. Sometimes, it failed to save me from my situation.

3.6 The Watermelon Garden and the Little Sparrow

Are not two sparrows sold for a cent? And yet not one of them will fall to the ground apart from your Father. But the very hairs of your head are all numbered.
Matthew 10: 29-30

I was eating brown rice and kimchi when I heard my name called. "Joong Ki. Joong Ki! I've been looking everywhere for you. Here, try this!" My best friend Seong-ho put a piece of fruit in the palm of my hand. It was red with black seeds. I tried it. Oh wow, it was the sweetest and juiciest thing I had ever had in my life.

Seong-ho laughed. "I got it from the kitchen. Noona said it was not enough for everyone, so she didn't put it out. But she gave me a bit, and I wanted to share it with you," he said.

I said, "Thank you." Not only was he loyal and kind, but also generous to me. Since I enjoyed watermelon very much, I decided to plant some seeds in the garden in front of my cabin. Every day, I watered and nurtured the seeds. It made me proud to care for something.

One afternoon when I was attending my watermelon garden, a significant event happened. I saw a tiny bird fall from a tree. It was a brown and beige bird like a sparrow. He cried out in pain, and I could see his wing was hurt badly. I could see he was trying to breathe in and out. Compassion for the helpless hurt bird overtook me. I reached down to pick up the sparrow. His eyes were closed tightly, as if he trusted me to tend him back to health. I enveloped him with both my hands to make sure he was warm enough. I walked slowly to the cabin. I gave him water and some soft nuts. I made a nest of branches and leaves so the sparrow could rest. I made sure no animal was near to prey on him. These two incidents—tending my garden and caring for the sparrow— would later display important values in my life.

3.7 Angels Around Me

For He will give His angels charge concerning you,
To guard you in all your ways.
Psalm 91: 11

Even though I didn't know God yet, and He allowed me to be an orphan, it is clear that He certainly never left nor forsook me. He sent angels in human form to help me. The Holt's Orphanage and Adoption Agency made sure all my documentation was prepared. As I mentioned previously, potential adoptive parents usually would be hesitant to adopt a child with little or no information. There were so many people at Holt who worked on different aspects of my documents. First, there was Mr. Seng Ku Kim. He applied for my certificate of orphanhood so I could be legal as an orphan. Another man, Mr. Hyo Jong Lee also got me my Ho Juk Deung Bon (family registration) with the chief officer of Dai Mun District Office so I could be registered there as an orphan.

Holt assigned a nurse, Nurse Choi, to make reports of my health. Nurse Choi made sure I went through all the important check-ups and evaluations. She took notes of everything: what I ate every day for breakfast, lunch, dinner, and snack; what time I woke up and went to sleep; details on hygiene; my personal disciplines, as well as my emotional health, mental health, and social life. I passed these tests with flying colors. I was underweight but had gained from 15 kgs to 18 kgs (41 lbs.). I was small and thin for a nine-year-old, but they figured that was just my body type. I was not lacking anything at all. I was full of energy. I was smart, alert, happy, and content.

Nurse Choi also compiled records of all my shots and immunizations together with my health reports. Mr. Lim collected my school records, my birth report, my certificate of orphanhood, and medical history. Then he wrote a recommendation for me to be adopted. I am glad they were thorough with all my required documents.

Finally, all my documents were in order. They handed my documents to be translated by an American doctor. Dr. Roth checked my temperature, weight, height, skin complexion, vision, bones, and teeth – basically everything. He observed how I walked, ran, played, and used my leg post-polio and surgery. Then he interviewed Noona and the orphanage workers about my eating habits, sleeping habits, toilet skills, and other things I was able to do.

Next, he made notes on how I interacted with adults, like with the caregivers, Noona, and school teachers. He recorded how I played with my friends, how I understood instructions, and how I took care of my duties and responsibilities. He was impressed that I was well-developed emotionally, after going through so much, including having polio and surgery. He noticed I was sensitive (the first child progress report mentioned this too). It said I shed tears very easily, but in general I was very adaptable and mature. I related well with adults and my peers, so I would be a great candidate for adoption.

He was pleased that my Korean birth and health documents were complete and accurate. He then created a pre-flight child report. Months continued to go by. More child progress reports were done on my behalf. Each time the report would highly recommend me to be adopted. I didn't know any of these reports were being prepared on my behalf.

3.8 American Seeds

I will not leave you as orphans; I will come to you.
John 14: 18

It was interesting how God planted seeds of faith about America when I was in the foster home before. I watched that American air show and was mesmerized by it. Since then, I was aware of this group of strange people who didn't look like us. I didn't understand who they were, where they came from, or what they were doing there, but I had a good feeling about them that I couldn't explain.

When I encountered more Americans in the orphanage, I felt my heart easily warmed toward them. It was so pleasant to get to know a few Americans, like Molly and Grandma Bertha. I was also excited to see more American military people. One time, we all gathered down at the large playing field area, and a military helicopter descended onto the field. Of course, seeing an American soldier, and especially the huge flying machine up close was immensely exciting. This friendly American soldier came out carrying cases of Coca-Cola® to share with us. I didn't know what it was, but I knew it was some kind of drink. When I tried Coca-Cola® that first time, I spewed it out of my mouth. I couldn't stand it at all! The fizzy dark brown drink was too harsh on my throat. I never tried it again until several years later in America.

Another fond feeling about America was from this story. One time, our house mom gathered us all together and presented a package from America from one of the boys who had been adopted recently by a family in Texas. I remember my friends and I were amazed at the luxurious life this boy was living now, as he was able to send us gifts.

To my surprise, one day my house mom asked me, "Joong Ki, would you like to be adopted and go live with an American family in the US?"

I thought for a minute, *everyone else is doing it so why shouldn't I?* I replied "Ok, why not, everyone else is doing it."

I was nine years old going on 10, and I liked the idea of being adopted. Although I had loved my friends and my life in the orphanage, one by one my friends would be adopted too. I continued the rest of the year by going to school, playing with friends, doing the chores, and having more physical examinations. The Holt angels were diligently observing me, making sure I was healthy in every way and lacked nothing. They continued taking me for health tests, progress on my visa at the American Consul, and making tons of reports.

By August's child progress report, I was matched with the Johns family in Michigan. When they told me that a family in America wanted to adopt me, I had no feelings either way. On the one hand, I was happy living at Holt Orphanage in Ilsan; the people had become my family. On the other hand, I thought being adopted into a family of my own was good also. I got my picture taken in front of the trees with a clean white shirt and dark shorts with a tag on my shirt bottom listing my name and ID number.

I knew that I would leave as soon as all the preparations were made for the adoption. I asked my friend Seong-ho to tend the watermelon I had planted and to nurture my little bird to health. These were very important to me. I felt like I was leaving a bit of myself in that orphanage. In other words, I felt I would want my friends to remember me through the watermelon and the bird.

"I promise," Seong-ho said to me. I hugged him tightly.

"Thank you, Seong-ho. You're my best friend. I hope you'll be adopted soon."

He nodded. I never saw him again, but from time to time I'd remember him and our friendship memories.

CHAPTER

04

A New Life in America

"'For I know the plans that I have for you,' declares the Lord, 'plans for welfare and not for calamity to give you a future and a hope. Then you will call upon Me and come and pray to Me, and I will listen to you. You will seek Me and find Me when you search for Me with all your heart.'"
Jeremiah 29:11-13

4.1 The Plaid Bag

The Lord is the one who goes ahead of you; He will be with you.
He will not fail you or forsake you. Do not fear or be dismayed.
Deuteronomy 31: 8

"Joong Ki, now remember, this is your bag," Noona had to say again, although she knew I was so good at taking care of my belongings. I had borderline OCD with keeping my things neat and organized. Noona met me one day before my departure date, and gave me a multi-colored, plaid bag. Noona had written in big marker letters "Juhn Joong Ki" on one side near the handle and my new American name "David Israel Johns" on the other side. I was just quiet. I think I might have been a little sad, knowing I would probably not see her nor my friends again, especially my best friend Seong-ho. I just suppressed it as usual because it was better not to be so sad and cry again.

"Joong Ki. Take your bag." Noona touched my hand again. I guess I froze looking at my plaid bag. *All my possessions would be in just this one bag.* I hugged it immediately.

"Now, do you still remember the two words I taught you?" her voice was sober.

I nodded. "물 mul (water); 어머니 omeoni (mommy)." The second word was easier to say. "Mommy" sounded like "Omeoni."

"You've always been a smart boy and a good boy. I'll miss you, Joong Ki." Noona 's voice cracked.

I hugged Noona one last time. Molly was my momma angel. My big sister. My nurse. My encourager. I didn't know who Mother Teresa was at the time, but Molly could be called the Mother Teresa of Korea for what she had done for the Korean orphans. She devoted her life to caring and advocating for the unwanted children – orphaned or abandoned. She defended the most forgotten, those with developmental problems or physical needs like my handicap from polio. She loved us like her own children, but she knew if the organization could match us with loving families who would adopt us, we would thrive even better. If Koreans weren't seeing children with medical needs, developmental problems, or physical handicaps as adoptable, then

American families might. Molly would fight for the Holt organization's primary tenet, that every child deserves to be loved, accepted, and part of a family.

When I left, the air was crisp and cold since we had to go very early in the morning. Several other children piled into the Toyota Land Cruiser™ that had jeep-like seats, including in the very back along the two side windows. I took my position in the back with my sole possession of that one plaid bag. We were off to the airport.

As I saw the huge passenger airplanes, I felt I could not get enough of them. Ever since I watched the American fighter jets bombing at the bay, I had fallen in love with airplanes. Now I was so excited to go on my first plane ride. My dream of riding in a jet airplane finally came true.

4.2 Coming to America

Behold, I am with you and will keep you wherever you go, and
will bring you back to this land; for I will not leave you until I
have done what I have promised you.
Genesis 28: 15

On the early morning ride to Gimpo International Airport in Seoul, I had brought my multi-colored plaid bag, and rehearsed in my head the two English words that Noona taught me. These were the most important two words a foreign child needed to know: water and mama.

Mr. David Kim (David Hyungbok Kim) took me all the way to America. He was another angel from the Lord. In order to fly all of us children from Korea to the USA, he had to become our legal guardian. He signed all of our immigration and adoption documents. I don't remember how many children were in the group who went with me, but mostly they were babies and little kids. Mr. David Kim was truly like a father to all of us. In the plane of 60-100 kids, he definitely didn't sleep. He helped change diapers, prepared milk, consoled crying babies to sleep, and then started the process again for the whole 10+ hours journey from Seoul to San Francisco, California.

I don't remember much of the trip except I loved flying. It didn't seem to scare me. I was fascinated by the clouds. I was amazed that this huge plane that was able to carry a group of more people than I'd ever seen in my life could fly above the clouds. I looked out the window until I got sleepy. I slept so long in the plane; I must have been so tired. I didn't hear babies crying. I woke up only when the stewardess served the meal. Oh wow! Such nice food on a pretty tray. I really enjoyed eating on the plane. I ate quietly and made sure I didn't leave any mess. I was already a neat boy anyway. Besides, I knew Mr. David Kim was already so tired attending to all the babies. He was counting on me to be a responsible and independent boy and I didn't want to bother him. My winning formula to be smart, strong, and independent kicked in nicely, but also, deep inside I was really busy soaking in all the new and fun experiences. So much soaking made me fall asleep again.

When I woke up the second time, we were nearing coastal waters. The ten-hour plane ride went by quickly. It was so fortunate that it was a sunny day. Usually, San Francisco would be cloudy and foggy around that time. I looked out the window and saw hundreds of ships big and small. There were many commercial and sailing boats cruising and crowding along the bay. Later, the pilot announced that we were landing in San Francisco.

When we landed, someone was already waiting for all who came from Holt. We were escorted to a special room where those of us who could read were given a rose colored, hand-sized Korean to English dictionary. I was glad to receive that dictionary. It was small enough for me to carry everywhere, and it would help me learn English.

After a few hours, Mr. Kim and I headed off to Michigan on another commercial airline. I didn't know where the other babies were taken, but everything had been arranged so that Mr. Kim would continue to fly with me. That was all that was important to me at the time. I held on to my plaid bag and followed his steps. If he walked fast, I tried to walk fast too. I don't remember if we had any conversation. He was very focused on finishing the trip with me, to hand me off, so he could take care of the other children. I understood. I didn't raise myself to be demanding. So, I just followed and soon was on the plane with him to Michigan.

When we landed in Michigan, I met the entire Johns family, six in all: mom, dad, one boy and three girls. The boy's name was Billy, and I was to be his companion. I saw Mr. Kim talk with the father and mother, and then he called me in Korean, "Joong Ki. Come here." I came obediently to him. He bent down to hug me and said his goodbye. I hugged him and then I went with the family. We piled into a long station wagon and headed to my new home, a three-story house in the country.

It was very overwhelming. I was in a new country, and everyone looked like the Americans I'd met in Korea. I didn't understand the language. I wasn't used to the food. They didn't have kimchi, but they had rice. It was the first time in my life that I saw white rice. These strangers were supposed to be my family now. I had a new home, a new family, and a new bedroom to share with the little boy, yet strangely, I felt more alone than ever. Mr. David Kim wasn't with me, and I didn't have anything familiar except my plaid bag. I didn't know how to process these mixed feelings.

That night, I was officially entering the folds of the Korean adoptees diaspora, leaving my homeland, culture, language, and history. I was no longer this Korean orphan named Juhn Joong Ki, case number 7253. I was now David Israel Johns. I felt strange and alone, but the Lord's eyes never departed from me.

4.3 A New Family

For the eyes of the Lord move to and fro throughout the earth that He may strongly support those whose heart is completely His.
2 Chronicles 16: 9a

When I arrived in Michigan, it was sometime in early September. Immediately, I noticed the stunning display of autumn leaves in reds, oranges, and golds. The fabulous fall trees blanketed the hills, streets, and roads. This made me enjoy being outside. The weather was like what I was used to in Korea.

We lived on several acres of farmland in a big, three-story country house that was like a mansion. The backside of the house was graced with green grass and rows of fabulous trees. A country road turned into a long, dirt driveway to our house. We had neighbors, but we were separated by a long, wood fence. The nearest neighbor's house was also on many acres and was a ten minute walk.

In the beginning, I remember my life with this family being happy. I was usually a content boy wherever I was and adapted to life wherever I was assigned. I didn't want to get into any trouble. I knew in the orphanage we had the house mom, Molly, Mr. David Kim, and other adults who supervised us. Here in this foreign land, I had no one else. I had to make it work. I really thought everything would be going okay. I tried hard to become part of the new family. They seemed to accept me. I learned a bit of English from playing and observing. I also picked up on the routines the family set out for me.

I remember waking up in the morning to get ready. Soon I would be going to school on a yellow school bus with the other kids. The bus driver picked us up all the way out on the rolling hills of the country road. Our neighboring kids hopped on the bus too, down the road a hundred yards away from us.

Really, the only thing I remember about school was the singing class. We sang one song, *Do-Re-Mi*© from the *Sound of Music*©. It quickly became my favorite song. The words were too fast, and I didn't understand them, but I really enjoyed singing the tunes as much as I could.

And riding home on the yellow school bus, kids teased my new brother singing:

"Oh, where have you been, Billy Boy, Billy Boy?
Oh, where have you been, Charming Billy?"

I really liked the joyful tune of that song. I didn't understand the meaning of the words but it was funny to see Billy's reactions. He was sheepishly smiling, so the song must have been pretty silly and a bit embarrassing to him, but I only remembered the "Billy Boy, Billy Boy" part. Those two songs are stuck in my memory forever. I'm sure we did a lot more than that at school, but being brand new in America with only two words to my ownership, the rest of school was a blur.

Of course, like any other kid, I played at school. I rode the merry-go-round, swung on the swings, and bravely tried to ride a bicycle. I learned new games and new ways. I never played any of these American games at Holt Ilsan Orphanage.

I remember the mom bought me some new clothes. The outfit I especially remember was a tan two-piece vest and pants with a white shirt to be worn on nice occasions. She also took me to the town to have a doctor do a full checkup. The doctor confirmed that I didn't need to get new vaccinations, since I had already completed those in Korea.

For some reason, the health clinic made an impression on me. It was located on the side of the town that had beautiful streets. I was so mesmerized by the sight of huge, gorgeous trees on each side of the street, arching their branches to make a tree tunnel and a continuous canopy overhead. I loved seeing these streets.

Several times we piled into the station wagon and went to see the grandparents. I don't remember much about those visits, except riding in the back of the wagon with the kids as we rode up and down the rolling hills.

I remembered going to some sort of church or maybe a synagogue for a religious service. Someone was yelling at the front of the rectangular hall, and we sat way in the back. I only remember going there once. I'm not sure which religion the family was, except in the third story of the house, there was a three-tiered statue of David from the Old Testament that symbolized the three periods of David's life. The statue of David could be rotated.

When I first arrived, the mom didn't ask if I knew how to bathe. I actually knew how to bathe, and I was toilet trained. I was innately a very clean person so personal hygiene was important to me. Also, in the orphanage we had to clean and fold our own bed and do many house cleaning routines. But how could I explain all that in English? So, I just let her bathe me. She also had the older sister bathe me if she wasn't able to. I just hoped they would understand quickly that I was good at these routines.

The older sister gave me a small, red photo album to save pictures in. I didn't have a camera, but the family gave me some pictures.

The dad "brought home the bacon," and it must have been a big bacon, since the mom stayed home to take care of the four kids, now five.

September passed and October came. In Michigan, October was already turning frigid, especially the nights. Halloween was only weeks away. Then it happened.

4.4 "JESUS!"

As for me, I shall call upon God, And the Lord will save me.
Psalm 55: 16

The October night that would forever change my life happened without warning. The dad was working a graveyard shift at the auto plant, and the mom was away for the night. The other kids had invited some friends over to play. We all played and played. When the mom came home, some of the kids blamed me for something that I didn't do, or at least not purposely. The mom was so furious, she dragged me down to the basement and started to stack paint cans on top of another – three in all. I didn't know what was going on. I didn't understand what she was screaming at me. I knew I must have done something very terrible.

She stripped all my clothes off and then put me on top of the stacked tower of cans. Then she forced me to grab full paint cans, one in each hand. That was my punishment for something I was accused of doing. To this day, I don't know what my infraction was. I was sobbing as I stood there until I couldn't hold on to the cans anymore. As if that was not enough, the mom somehow got my one lone possession, the plaid bag, and dragged me out into the dark, night air. She pushed the bag into my hand and screamed, "I'm sending you back to Korea!" There I stood bawling my eyes out holding my bag in the cold, dark night. I only wanted to be accepted in this new land and by this family. I just wanted to please them.

In that moment of self-pity, I thought the only person who might come to my rescue was the dad. I imagined walking out to the end of the long driveway and putting myself in my little bag. When the dad came home, he would see me in the bag and have pity on me. All I wanted was to be accepted.

I knew that wouldn't work and then I suddenly remembered at Holt's Orphanage they told me about Jesus. I never knew Him or asked Him into my life, but suddenly, out of total desperation, I cried out loudly "JESUS!"

The mom eventually let me back into the house.

After that night everything changed. Everyone in that house treated me like a weird person. The other kids didn't console me. I was alone, confused, scared, ashamed, dejected, and full of despair. I was an outcast. I didn't have enough vocabulary to articulate my thoughts. I didn't know what to do. I was stuck. I knew Korea was far away. I didn't know who to call. I didn't know where Mr. David Kim was, and even if he was near, how could I ask for his help? I didn't know how to get hold of him. I felt alone, confused and helpless. I was so afraid every day. What if the mom really kicked me out next time? I couldn't explain or ask questions or get the dad to hear my story. The children didn't dare to defend me, play with me, or become my friends again. They were supposed to be my siblings. Every day was full of heaviness and sadness.

Since that day, the abuse manifested in different forms, although, I didn't know they were forms of abuse. The mom would put a mirror in front of me and tell me to walk up the staircase. She told me to "walk normally, walk normally." She taunted me for not knowing how to walk normally. Well, I didn't know how to walk "normally" because I limped from polio. I walked funny. I ran funny. That was just how it was. After that, I hated stairs.

When Halloween came, the mom dressed me like a girl with girl's stockings, a fancy tutu dress, a wig, and everything. I was so horrified at the thought. With tears and pleading eyes, I showed her my reluctance. I was so ashamed. I was 10. I knew I was a boy, not a girl. This was so embarrassing. But she proceeded to take me "trick or treating" from house to house. I abhorred the entire incident.

She also forced me to wear diapers to school. I was very young when I was potty trained. All my documents and progress reports had that section about toileting. I never had any accidents at home nor at school. But she wanted to humiliate me, although I didn't know what that word meant. I just knew I felt so bad for having to wear them. It was not comfortable, and my pants bulged from it. I just tried to go along with it, since I had no one to talk to about what was happening. It never crossed my mind to report or tell anyone about what the family did to me. I just wanted to be accepted and for everything to work out. I didn't need to be loved, just accepted. Well, when I cried, "JESUS" that night in October, the Lord was listening and was already at work to send me my miracle.

Another month passed with this family. It must have been late November or early December when the mom told me I would be going to another family, but I would be put in the orphanage until the family was ready. After that decision was settled, the mom was actually nicer to me. She taught me how to wash hands properly the American way and other manners. When I left that family, I didn't have any tears.

70

The family sent me away with some clothes and the red picture album. For several weeks, I was housed at an orphanage in Michigan. It was during Christmas. I remembered the cold snow falling and how I played happily in the snow with the other kids. I didn't know who my next family would be, but I was so relieved I wasn't with that first family anymore. I didn't harbor bitterness or hate. I still thought I did something wrong. I blamed myself for not knowing what went wrong and not being able to explain it in English. But now it was behind me. I was free to play, and I wanted to enjoy the moment. For Christmas, I chose an American football game to take when I continued on my journey to the next home.

By this time, I was used to moving from place to place and home to home. Up to that point, that was my life. I didn't know the words "abuse" and "rejection," but the trauma of experiencing them caused my brain to suppress memories of my Korean past and the Johns family. I was successful at suppressing them to the point that I was losing my Korean language at a fast rate, and I couldn't remember many details about my Korean heritage. In fact, I still can't remember much of my past and the Johns family, except what I have written in this book. I subconsciously blocked those painful memories to preserve myself and move on. It would be later and take many years for the Lord to start doing the unlocking in me.

CHAPTER

05

A Brand-New Chapter

Therefore, if anyone is in Christ, he is a new creation.
The old has passed away; behold, the new has come.
2 Corinthians 5:17 ESV

5.1 New Mercies Every Morning

The steadfast love of the LORD never ceases; His mercies never come to an end; they are new every morning; great is your faithfulness.
Lamentations 3:22-23 ESV

The day finally came! Mr. David Kim picked me up from the temporary orphanage. When he showed up at the door, a sense of comfort came over me because I recognized his familiar face; there was the same kind and fatherly guardian who had brought me over from Korea just a few months prior. My face couldn't hide my happiness. I hugged him tightly. With a big smile, he told me a new family was waiting for me in Oregon.

I didn't know how to process my experience with the Johns family. I had a hard time understanding what had happened. Deep inside, I had feelings of guilt and shame as if the incidents of abuse were my fault. I didn't know how to identify them. I just wanted to bury them in the deepest abyss so they would never resurface. But Mr. David Kim helped me feel secure and safe enough to try again with another family. I had no choice anyway, except to trust him, and my winning formula said I needed to be tough, to make things work, and not cause any problem. My winning formula said I shouldn't grieve and entertain self-pity but move on and not cause any trouble. So, I braced myself, and together we went to the airport to fly from Michigan to Oregon.

We landed in a small airport in Eugene, Oregon. Mr. Kim held my hand down the airplane stairway, across the short tarmac, and into the gate area. We were greeted by a smiling middle-aged couple. The husband was a tall, bald-headed man with black glasses and blue eyes, while his wife was a blue-eyed, gleaming-mouthed, blondish-grayish-haired woman. I was shy. I just looked at them. Somehow in my eyes they looked kind and loving, not scary and intimidating like the first family in Michigan.

Then something magical happened. While we were awkwardly sitting down to get used to one another, the man saw my boxed football game. He asked if I wanted to play. I gladly agreed, and so we played. I was so happy that the man would play with me. Right away, I knew this couple was the genuine family I was promised when I was at Holt Ilsan Orphanage.

Again came the farewell. Mr. David Kim hugged me, kissed my forehead, and gave me my faithful plaid bag. I waved good-bye to Mr. David Kim. He talked a little bit with the man and the woman, and then he was gone.

Although I didn't have much memory of Mr. Kim except the travels from Korea to Michigan and from Michigan to Oregon, I always felt a strong connection to him. I felt he was truly a guardian to me, rescuing me from the first family and bringing me to this new family in Oregon. My life would have been different had he not advocated for me. I only met Mr. David Kim one more time when he checked on me in elementary school. (I guess our reunion will have to be in Heaven, since he passed on in 2018).

My new mom and dad guided me out of the airport arrival gate to the parking lot where their truck, a white Ford F-150™, was waiting. We all sat across the only seat available, with my dad at the driver's seat, my mom in the middle, and me by the window. I looked out my window into the night sky with a partial view of the moon overhead hiding behind a light cloud. We stopped to get a grape soda drink at a roadside convenience store.

I was so happy that I was singing the whole drive home from the Eugene airport to Roseburg, Oregon. In less than an hour, I arrived at my new home with the Pearman family.

5.2 A Powerful Dream

Indeed God speaks once,
Or twice, yet no one notices it.
In a dream, a vision of the night,
When sound sleep falls on men,
While they slumber in their beds.
Job 33: 14-15

Many years later, my mom recalled to me the story of how they had tried for almost ten years to adopt a four-year-old Korean boy. Here's her side of the story in her own words:

"In February 1962, I was baptized as a believer of Jesus Christ. Just a few months later, I saw a program on television about a family named Holt, who started an orphanage in Korea. The Holts had gone through a lot of red tape and adopted several Korean/American orphans themselves. And the Holts were Christians.

"Shortly thereafter, a friend loaned me a book written by Bertha Holt entitled *Seed from the East*, and a desire to adopt a little Korean boy was planted in my heart. My husband Don and I had two little girls already, but Don said 'no' to adopting a boy. He was not a Christian, so his heart was not ready for something that serious.

"During the years that followed, I'd just about forgotten about adopting a child, then I'd see a Korean boy, or a mother of adopted Koreans, and my heart would be nudged to remember my own desire to adopt.

"Finally, my husband grew tired of my nagging, and said, 'If I get a promotion at the post office, we'll adopt a boy.' But there was no promotion, and I kept on nagging.

"In 1970, my husband relented on the condition that I save the money, about $600 [in 1970, on average a man working full time would make $9180/year. Rent was $108/month, groceries were $50/month, and gas was $0.36 per gallon]. So saving $600 was a real challenge, because we weren't people that saved five dollars a month. But I prayed, started saving all of my babysitting earnings, and the Lord blessed it. From April to December, I'd saved $600. I hadn't kept my husband informed of my financial progress. When I told him I'd saved that much money, he was very surprised, but he was not ready to adopt. But he had a good idea. He said, 'Why don't we send a birthday present to Jesus?' On December 24th, we mailed a check for $600 to the Holt orphanage office, specifying that it be used to place a child in a loving Christian home.

"When the receipt came back, the money had been put in the general fund. The receipt had various 'slots' the money could have been put in, and when I saw the general fund had a check mark, I cried.

"My husband, Don said, 'Alright, don't cry. If you really want to adopt a child that badly, go ahead and save another $600.' And this time I knew it could be done.

"Again, the Lord blessed my efforts, and by the end of September 1971, there was another $600 in savings. A surprise for Don, but this time he said, 'I'm not sure if this is God's will or your will; and if it's God's will, He is going to have to show me.' We talked it over and decided Don needed confirmation from the Lord by Christmas time.

"Two weeks went by and then it happened. Don said he never dreamed (since he was a light sleeper), but one night he dreamed and remembered it. [Let me say that dreams aren't always used by the Lord. Some dreams are senseless. But there are Scriptural records of times when the Lord revealed His will in dreams.] The next morning my husband very happily told me he had a dream.

"In the dream, Don saw himself standing on a riverbank, and the water was dark brown, dirty and turbulent. Floating by was a little boy bobbing up and down in the water, and Don knew he had to rescue the child. Don reached out with one hand and rescued him. As he pulled the child from the water, he saw the boy had a little round, Oriental face. And he heard a voice say, 'You have two hands, use them both.' Don believed that was a sign from God. [This was most likely the same night David cried out "Jesus!" on that fateful, cold, dark, October night in Michigan.]

"After this, Don was 'gung-ho' to adopt. We filled out an application and sent a $50 check to show our sincerity. We each had to write a testimony of our faith in Jesus Christ.

"We made several trips to Creswell, Oregon to the orphanage office to talk to case workers, and we had a home visit from one of the staff. We had applied for a four-year-old boy, and the orphanage suggested we take an older child, because of our ages. But I said no.

77

"The family discussed what we'd name our child, and we came up with John David, two good Biblical names. The orphanage said it would possibly be six months before we'd get our child.

"But the Lord worked things out differently. We got a phone call shortly after Christmas saying there was a Korean boy already in the United States, but he wasn't working out with his American family. He was 10 years old, but would we consider taking him on a trial basis?

"Don and I scurried around buying a bed, and with the help of our daughters, we furnished a bedroom.

"On January 5th, 1972, Don and I drove to Eugene to pick up our boy. This too was a small miracle, because most potential parents had to go to Seattle or San Francisco to get their child.

"When David got off the airplane, he said, 'Hi,' and I took his hand. When Don and I, David, and the case worker (who'd traveled with David) went inside the airport, we saw the name on the bag that held all of the boy's earthly belongings. I was shocked; it was labeled 'David Israel Johns.' The name we'd planned was John David. We decided to leave his name as it was, until we officially adopted him and changed his last name. I knew this was the boy God wanted us to have.

"I asked the case worker how much money we still owed the orphanage. He replied, 'Nothing.' The check we'd sent them for Christmas in 1970 had truly been used to 'place one child in a loving, Christian home.' Our home.

"We still had $550 in savings. The Lord soon gave me a ministry using that money.

"And that year, 1972, my husband didn't get one promotion; the Lord blessed him with two. Praise the name of Jesus!

"After we picked David up at the airport and drove home, my oldest daughter had come home from work. As I was fixing dinner, she and Don were helping David get settled in and she came into the kitchen crying. Alarmed, I asked, 'Patti, what's the matter?' Through her tears she said, 'Nothing! I just know this is the child God wants you to have.'

"That had been many years ago, and we all agree David was the child God wanted us to have."

To announce the arrival of their newly adopted boy, my parents ran a short notice in the *Roseburg Gazette Times* that read from the copy of the original clipping:

"We CHOSE this way to thank the many people who prayed or showed interest in our getting our Korean boy. His name is David and he's 10 years old.

We just marvel at how Christ brought this particular boy to us! David is fantastic, and we sincerely believe Christ guided the whole procedure.

We especially thank all the children! They have so warmly welcomed David.

In Christ, we are – The Pearmans"

After my parents adopted me, they received invitations to talk about my adoption, from churches to radio talk shows. My mom always said yes to these, as she hoped my adoption story would inspire a lot of people to do the same. Adoption is God's way to bless both parents and children.

5.3 Assimilation: Becoming a Pearman, an American

And it shall be that in the place where it was said to them, 'you are not My people,' There they shall be called sons of the living God.
Romans 9:26

I got up the next morning to the sound of kids' voices. Where did the kids come from? Lo and behold, I learned that my new mom's job was to take care of kids of all ages, from toddlers to early teens. Lots of kids. Maybe there were over 10 kids throughout the day. I had instant friends to play with. Even though I didn't know the English language that well yet, I knew the language of play.

My dad worked for the post office. He was quite a handyman. We lived in a humble, three-bedroom corner home with a driveway that came down from the street, and there was a wrap-around hilly yard on two sides. He saw that I was happy playing with the kids, so he decided to spoil us children by making a little graveled playground with swings and a two-story fort. The fort had spy holes around various points in the four walls and stairways on two sides of the front. My mom asked for a big white cross in front of the fort. We really enjoyed playing with the new swings in our playground and creating fun stories from our imaginations.

Another time, Dad moved a whole interior wall to expand the playroom and shortened his shop by himself. I was engulfed with so much emotion, seeing how kind and accommodating my dad was to me and my friends. My dad and I bonded almost immediately.

My mom took care of us really well too. Being the main disciplinarian, she instilled in us manners and godly values like kindness and compassion. For example, she always said that everyone was special in God's eyes, and He loved each child the same. She would never tolerate bullying behavior, disrespectful attitudes, or unkind words in the house. My friends, being children, didn't seem to care so much that I walked differently because I had polio, that my skin and face looked different than theirs, and that I couldn't speak much English yet. They sincerely accepted me and always wanted to play with me. Every day I waited for them to be dropped off, so I could play with them.

We had such fun adventures. On the days that my mom had to do grocery shopping, she'd put all of us in the car and off we'd go. These were the days when seatbelt rules weren't established yet, so the six of us kids would sit in the second row of the car. Sometimes she'd treat us to ice cream cones, and we'd eat them in the car. One time my mom was turning a corner a bit too fast, and one girl flew out of the car. She was bruised, but her hand was still holding her ice cream cone steadily. We had a good laugh about that for many years to come.

My mom was so smart and creative linguistically. She'd gather us and prompt each of us for nouns, adjectives, adverbs, and verbs. Then she'd make up a story on the spot. They were always funny. She always included each of us, and used the nouns, adjectives, adverbs, and verbs that we chose earlier creating a beautiful, moving but funny story. We had many good laughs in the car, in the living room, in the yard, or wherever she started this game. We could never get bored because of her creativity. I think she'd be hired by Mad Libs in a heartbeat if they happened to know her. She was so brilliant. As she aged, she played Scrabble™ and other word games until she was too weak.

My parents' unconditional love and my friends' acceptance gave me such security and helped me thrive in my new environment. I assimilated into American culture and identity really smoothly. I started seeing myself as one of them. We lived on the corner of Jacobson Street and Brooklyn Avenue. Soon, I was known as "David Israel Pearman who lived on Jacobson Street." Later, I thought that to be coincidentally humorous and appropriate Biblically since Jacob's name was changed to Israel by God.

5.4 Losing My First Language and Acquiring a New One

And God is able to make all grace abound to you, so that always having all sufficiency in everything, you may have an abundance for every good deed;
2 Corinthians 9: 8

Play is the international language of kids. I really don't know when I learned English. I don't remember trying to learn English. I must have just picked up the grammar and words along the way. I learned English as I played with the babysitting kids and the neighborhood kids. I learned English as we ran around outside, and played tag, fort, hide and seek, kickball on the street, basketball, or with Legos™. I learned as we played.

It's interesting that many people think internationally adopted children will become bilingual naturally. Yes, I think proficiency in the first language or mother language does provide a scaffolding to learn the second language. It helps them learn a second language faster. However, experts have found that unless the adopted children are intentionally given the opportunity to learn both languages, the birth language will easily stop, in fact, almost immediately.

There are two important reasons for this. First of all, most adoptive parents do not speak the birth language of the adopted child. Second, when the adopted child begins to learn the new adopted language (or the second first language), he or she is not mature yet in the language development of the birth language. So when it stops prematurely, it is hard to retrieve it. Dr. Boris Gindis, a famous adoption psychologist from Russia, noted that Russian children adopted from ages four to eight lost expressive use of their language within three to six months of adoption and all functional use of the language within a year. In short, internationally adopted children are only bilingual for a very short window of time after adoption.

This happened to me. In a matter of a few months to a year, I lost my ability to communicate in Korean, including speaking, understanding, reading, and writing. It could be because I was trying hard to adapt to the new culture and language for my survival. My winning formula to be smart, strong, and independent took over, so I was determined to learn English. In addition, my Korean language development experienced a premature halt from not being nourished in any way. I had no one to converse with in Korean in my little town, and I had no interest or need to find another Korean adoptee to help me survive my new environment. That thought never occurred to me. Later, I learned the scientific name for this premature halt is "arrested language development."

I didn't mourn the loss of my birth language, but because I was proficient enough in Korean, it provided a nice scaffolding for me to learn a new language. Without trying, my brain absorbed new vocabulary like a sponge. If my typical six -year-old friends already understood over 20,000 English words, as a freshly adopted child from Korea, I needed to learn an average of 54 new words every day in order to catch up on language comprehension abilities in one year. If the catch-up timeframe was stretched out to two years, I still needed to learn an average of 27 new words each day to fully catch up by age 12. However, while I was busy playing catch-up, my six -year-old friends also added an average of 5,000 words to their vocabulary. When my friends turned seven, they'd understand 25,000 words. With this addition I needed to learn an average of 34 words per day to reach the same developmental level within two years. According to this simple calculation, I probably developed progressively proficient English language skills within two years of my adoption.

After two years, I was able to speak quite fluently with very minimal accents and was proud of it. I was happy to connect with my family and friends for day-to-day social interactions and understand contextual cues, even though I hadn't mastered full comprehension of the language yet. This level of English helped my cognitive and linguistic skills develop nicely. I think the correct terminology for this is BICS Fluency. BICS stands for Basic Interpersonal Communication Skills.

Once I started school, academic learning helped me acquire all vocabulary and grammar concepts necessary to have full language proficiency in an academic setting. After being in school for a few years, my level of English proficiency went up to the academic level, also known as CALPS – Cognitive Academic Language Proficiency. I was proud to have an American accent because I wanted so much to be seen as an American.

Soon, I forgot not only my Korean language but also my roots and traditions. My memories became intermittent, preserved for specific incidents only and not a continuous narrative of events. I believe my brain decided to block my childhood memories for two reasons: I didn't want to relive the painful childhood traumas, and my winning formula continued to drive me to assimilate into the new culture. Deep inside my heart, I just wanted to become an American boy as soon as possible. I was now David Israel Pearman and this was forever. Juhn Joong Ki was my past. I was no longer him and would never be again. I would reject not only my Korean roots, but anything and everything —related to being Asian. I was an American boy, just like my new family and my friends. In fact, later, I took a big, black marker and blocked out my Korean name and the last name of the Michigan family. Although I physically tried to erase all my Korean heritage, my nunchi —that sixth sense— would stay with me forever as my friend and my foe. As a friend, my nunchi kept me out of trouble within my social circles. As a foe, my feelings were overly sensitive at times. Maybe that's why I cried easily as a young boy when somebody carelessly said something about me. Later as an adult, I realized it was a gift of discernment in my daily life.

CHAPTER

06

God is Doing a New Thing

Do not call to mind the former things,
Or ponder things of the past.
Behold, I will do something new,
Now it will spring forth;
Will you not be aware of it?
I will even make a roadway in the wilderness,
rivers in the desert.
Isaiah 43: 18-19

6. 1 New Family Members

A friend loves at all times,
And a brother is born for adversity.
Proverbs 17: 17

School didn't begin right away for me, since my mom and dad thought it would be better for me to start fresh in September, at the start of the new school year, instead of midterm in January. I spent my days playing with friends and adjusting to my new life in Roseburg, Oregon. There were many new things I learned and experienced besides learning English and playing new games. I also got to know my family members.

First, I got to know my two sisters. My eldest sister, Patti, had already moved out to live on her own. Patti was very sweet. She adored me right away. She was very organized. She loved gardening and working with her hands. My other sister, Paula, had also moved out of the house already because she was married. Paula looked like my mom. Paula also loved me and interacted a lot with me. In fact, she already had a baby named Daniel, who was born the year I was adopted. Paula would bring him to play with me often. I loved babysitting Daniel. We became constant buddies, although I am technically the uncle. Daniel is still my closest family member.

I settled into this family as an only child, but with older sisters. No one spoiled me. They loved me with the love of the Lord. When I needed to be disciplined, it was always out of love. I could tell the difference from the way the Johns family treated me. Still, I had a hard time being close to my mom, since she was a mother figure, and I was still traumatized by the first mom, the Johns mom. I couldn't feel affection for Mom and would have a hard time with this for a long, long time.

I never experienced trauma like that with the Pearman family. However, one day, when we were on our way to visit Paula, there was a slight mishap. My sister Patti had to slam on the brakes, and I was in the front seat looking at all the sights. Remember, those were the days when we didn't wear seat belts. I banged my head on the front dashboard. I could feel my head start to swell with a huge bump. I cried quite loudly, and so we headed back to the house to take care of my unfortunate bump. We planned to visit Paula at a later time. That was probably the worst accident in my welcome to Roseburg. After that incident all was well. When we finally made it to Paula's, the trip was fun, and I had a great time playing with Daniel.

Second, I met extended family members. After some time, my family ventured out to visit relatives farther away. It took three or four hours to get to my grandparents in the Yamhill/Carlton area. Grandma Evie and Grandpa Lloyd were from my dad's side. Actually, Grandma Evie had remarried after the death of her first husband, so Grandpa Lloyd was her second husband. We stayed at their single level, simple country house. We talked, ate, played games, and went to church on Sunday, where I fell asleep beside Grandpa Lloyd who always got me with his "no-see me" bugs that would pinch me now and again. I always fell for it but loved the trick. Of course, like in many grandparents' homes, there were those notorious grandfather clocks that would make a loud "gong" every hour on the hour. If it was not the grandfather clocks, it was the cuckoo clock that would come out of the clock home and cuckoo on the hour. I think I didn't sleep well, since every hour I woke up with the gong or cuckoo. All this was new and strange to get used to, especially during bedtime.

6.2 I Matter!

Thus says the Lord who made you
And formed you from the womb, who will help you.
Isaiah 44:2a

One summer morning my mom called me to the dining room.

"David, I've been thinking about your birthday," she said, smiling from ear to ear. "Wouldn't it be fun to have a birthday party?"

"What's a birthday party?" I was puzzled.

I had never had a birthday party in my life. At the orphanage, we had holiday celebrations but not individual birthdays. Also, in Korean culture, the Korean Lunar New Year (the same as Chinese Lunar New Year) is the time to celebrate everyone's birthday, since on that day, everyone is considered a year older. Even a child who was born the day before the New Year would already turn one year old on the Korean Lunar New Year.

"You were born on July 13th, David. Each year, when it gets to that day, you turn one year older. This year, July 13th falls on a Thursday, " Mom said, pointing to the calendar.

That was the first time I knew the concept of a birthday. I knew we did something special for Mom and Paula a few months back but I didn't know those celebrations were for birthdays, let alone that I would get to have a birthday celebration too.

"I think we'll have your party on Saturday, July 15, so that we can invite all your friends. And most importantly, Dad won't have to go to work on that day," Mom continued.

After that, I looked closely at the calendar and counted how many sleeps before the day would come. As July 13 came closer, my mom planned and prepared the details for my first ever birthday party. My mom invited my handful of friends from the neighborhood and babysitting friends. On my birthday, she put a bench table at the playroom near the garage. She arranged balloons, put a nice tablecloth on the table and a cake in the middle.

It was a simple celebration, but to me this meant my life *mattered!* My mom and dad showed that I mattered and that my birth was something to be celebrated. They always said I was a gift from God for them, so I started believing them. My life also mattered to my friends who came. I really had a great time. My mom created some games for us to play. Then it was time for the cake. My mom brought the cake to me, told me to make a wish and blow out the candles on the cake. We all ate the yummy cake. Then it was time for me to open the presents in the playroom. I got some toys and books.

My heart was full, and I felt so, so happy. Then my dad put something big on my lap. It was the last gift, and it was from my mom and dad.

"Open it, son," he said, with loving eyes. My mom looked giddy next to him.

I opened it eagerly. All eyes were on me. I felt shy but excited at the same time.

"Oh, thank you, Dad!" I exclaimed. It was a reel-to-reel tape recorder, a Sony TC-630™. I didn't know what it was for, but Dad showed me how it worked. A mic was attached to it, and if I pressed the button, it would allow me to record people's voices. I loved it immediately since it was a cool device. I think that was the start of my interest in electronic gadgets. I just dragged my new recorder around and recorded the happenings during the party. That was so fun. Everyone contributed their voices, and I enjoyed being a "reporter". I loved my perfect, favorite gift. That was the first and last birthday party I had during my growing up years, but I certainly have fond memories of that day.

Most important, I was no longer an abandoned, rejected orphan. I was not an accident. I didn't know my biological parents, but my birth was not an accident. God wanted me in this world. My Pearman family wanted me in this world. I mattered.

6.3 A New School

The fear of the Lord is the beginning of knowledge, but fools despise wisdom and instruction.
Proverbs 1: 7

To help prepare me for school in the fall, my parents enrolled me in summer school for a few months. Most kids enjoyed a long summer break, but since I hadn't been in school since November, summer school was my time to catch up. In the fall of 1972, I officially started school in Oregon in the second grade. I was placed three grades below what my grade level in Korea would have been. I didn't mind, since I was smaller, and my English then was just survival level.

Mrs. Wilson became my second-grade teacher at Riverside Elementary School in Roseburg, Oregon. Mrs. Wilson was tall and blondish-gray, and she talked with such kindness. I felt at ease with her immediately. Mr. Crain was the principal at the time. I didn't interact with him that much, except when I was introduced to him at the beginning of the school year. I learned to take a bus to school and back home. In the morning, I had to walk to the bus stop. Other children would come down the street to the main bus stop. Everyone was very nice to me, and soon we got to know one another pretty well. In the afternoon for some reason, the bus driver took us to the corner of the main block, then we all got out and walked to our homes. I didn't have anyone who bullied me even though I had that fear of someone hurting me or being rejected once in a while. It must have been the favor of God upon my life that I didn't realize yet.

Soon it was December, so we had winter break and Christmas. My first Christmas at the Pearmans was more than special. Even though I had Christmas time at the Michigan orphanage the year before, this was truly my first real Christmas in America with a family who loved me. I saw all kinds of Christmas lights in colors and whites, with Santa Claus and his reindeer and Frosty the Snowman. Some houses had manger scenes. In my heart, December was filled with goodness and excitement. At school, we even had Christmas decorations and shared Christmas cookies. At church, we had many festivities every Sunday of December. We had a special Taste of

Christmas one Sunday evening in the fellowship hall, where the grade level Sunday School classrooms opened up their separate moveable partition walls to reveal one large room. Church folks brought their special Christmas treats to share with everyone after the Sunday night service. Another Sunday, the church choir had a special Christmas cantata with the choir members dressed up as characters from the Bible. They would tell the Christmas story through song, dialogues, and narrations. Then every night our church sponsored a live nativity scene.

My dad was involved in the cantata with his booming bass voice and he also stood in the nativity scenes. One night, Mom drove me to see my dad garbed as one of the wise men in the scene. They had real hay, some plastic animals, and an angel standing above the manger building. I said, "Hi, Daddy," with a warm puff of air blowing out into the cold, December night. After several hours, another set of people would relieve them. We went into the fellowship hall after my dad's shift and drank some hot chocolate with the others who were needing to warm up from the frigid outdoors. The night that my dad played in the scene was Christmas Eve night. As I rode home with my dad in his pickup, he asked if I was excited to open presents under the Christmas tree in our living room. Of course, I was. When we got home, I quickly ran into the house and asked Mom if we could open presents. She said, "Yes of course, but first Daddy will read the Christmas story from the Bible." My dad opened the Bible to the book of Matthew and read with his warm, deep voice. I didn't understand all the words, but I understood the story, since it was repeated in Sunday Schools and in the cantata. Then, finally the presents. The one gift I remember was a Hot Wheels™ dual lane racetrack with shifters. I just loved that racetrack for many years as I raced with my friends who came over. Christmas time became my favorite time of the year.

After the holidays January came, which meant I had been a Pearman for a whole year. I had no idea it had been a year, but my parents took notice that I was growing and thriving.

After the second term, Mrs. Wilson, Mr. Crane, and my parents discussed whether or not to move me up to the third grade. After some discussion, they all agreed that I could handle the challenge. Mrs. Wilson and Mr. Crain must have felt I was advancing well enough to move ahead. Mrs. Smith was shorter and stouter than Mrs. Wilson, but she was just as caring. She used crutches, but I didn't know why. She really encouraged me to work hard on all subjects, especially English. Math was the easiest subject for me, which was expected since there was not much English besides the story problems.

And just like that, spring was over. At the end of my first complete year of school in America, Mrs. Wilson and Mrs. Smith gave me a present. They purchased swimming lessons at the YMCA for the summer. I was both delighted and trepidatious; delighted that they would be so thoughtful but fearful of what might happen in the water because I had never swum before. My mom took me to the swimming pool, and soon I was able to swim decently. I never really enjoyed swimming that much since I only could use one of my legs to power through the water. I learned to compensate for the lack of power by using my arms more. I especially didn't like it when I got water in my nostrils and felt like I was going to drown. I tried to stay afloat and propel myself on the shallow ends and close to the edges so I could quickly grab on. I persevered through the lessons, as I knew it would be a necessary skill to have in case of emergency. That was instilled in me somehow.

6.4 Knowing Jesus

It's in Christ that we find out who we are and what we are living for, part of the overall purpose He is working out in everything and everyone.
Ephesians 1:11–12 (MSG)

This is the most important part of this chapter! God was doing a new thing in my life, but most important, He was always working at my heart to know Him personally and intimately. I didn't know Him yet, although I cried out His Name, "JESUS" at my lowest point of life at the Johns' house in Michigan.

At the Pearman's home, we didn't miss church on Sunday mornings. We would wake up early to get ready for church. It was something to look forward to every week. We also came to church many other times, like on Wednesday evenings midweek meetings, and sometimes even on Sunday evenings for special services. All I knew was church life was not a once in a long while event but was lived out by my parents daily. Many times, I saw Dad and Mom arguing about something, then they would reconcile and forgive each other. If they were wrong, they asked for my forgiveness. Wow, I never thought parents would do that to a child.

I saw how much they loved and valued everybody. People would come over to our house many times for food, advice, prayer, and support. No matter how tired my mom and dad were, they never refused anyone. Many troubled young adults from Job Corps would spend Sundays with us. I didn't know Jesus intimately, but they made me want to follow Jesus.

Sunday School was always fun. As I attended Sunday School week after week, my love for singing grew along with an eagerness to learn the wonderful stories from the Bible. My mom also served in Sunday School. She was a silly and fun teacher and would make up songs, like the song from the Coca-Cola™ commercial at the time, *I'd Like To Teach The World To Sing©*, Jim Nabors' version, 1972.

The melody was so nice. Before I knew it, I was already humming the song. My creative mom changed the lyrics with Jesus-centered words and then taught it to all of us kids in Sunday Schools on the piano.

I'd like to tell the world today
About the great big love
What Jesus Christ has done for us
For all of you and me
I'd like to teach the world to know
That He died on the cross
So we all can be forgiven
When we receive His love
He's the real thing
What the world needs today
Jesus, the only way
He's the real thing
I'd like to see the world for once
All standing hand in hand
And hear them echo through the hills,
God's peace throughout the land.
He's the real thing
What the world needs today
Jesus, the only way
He's the real thing

Oh! All Sunday school kids would sing and dance, and after a few times, we were quite a musical team. Some got fancy with their dance movements. Some added twirls and clapped along with the beat. Some beat on the tables. Some created echoes of this part:

He's the real thing…. (Jesus is real) …

What the world needs today (all need Jesus!)

Jesus the only way (only One way)

He's the real thing (Yes, He is).

When she stopped playing on the piano, we shouted and begged: "Please, Mrs. Pearman, play it again, play it again." Then she'd let us sing two more times, but after that we had to sit and listen to the Bible story. Oh, it was so much fun.

My mom knew memorizing the Bible was a challenge for us, so she also made-up silly songs so we'd remember Bible verses easier. For example, she

94

was teaching about not being tempted to do things that God would not like. The memory verse was from 1 Corinthians 10:13, and it was so long:

"No temptation has overtaken you except as is common to man; but God is faithful, who will not allow you to be tempted beyond what you are able, but with the temptation will also make the way of escape, that you may be able to bear it."

But when we sang it to the tune of *His Banner Over Me Is Love*©, we all were able to memorize it. This was a practice that I kept until my adult years.

Since my heart was so tender and open to the Lord, I started noticing how some of the hymns we sang in the American church service sounded very similar to the songs we sang at the Korean orphanage. All those Christian songs didn't mean anything to me back then, but the Lord had planted them as seeds in the good soil of my heart. And we sang them in Korean back then. By this time, I couldn't remember the words anymore, but I still remembered the tunes. Now that I was singing them again in English, my heart was truly touched and the hymns became more than just songs. They fed my hungry soul in a precious way. One of them was *At the Cross*©

Alas, and did my Savior bleed and did my sovereign die
Would He devote that sacred head for such a worm as I
At the cross, at the cross, where I first saw the Light
And the burden of my heart rolled away, (rolled away)
It was there by Faith, I received my sight
And now I am happy all the day
Was it for crimes that I have done, He crawled up on the tree
Amazing pity, grace unknown and love beyond degree
At the cross, at the cross, where I first saw the Light
And the burden of my heart rolled away, (rolled away)
It was there by Faith, I received my sight
And now, I am happy all the day.

Remembering those songs gave me reassurance that God was taking care of me at the orphanage even before I knew Him. That was the start of me seeing Him as the Light. And soon, one-by-one, just like the refrain of the song said, those burdens—the pains and the griefs of being abandoned, rejected, and abused, all rolled away. I was happy, and I knew this happiness wasn't man-made. I didn't accept Jesus verbally yet, but I knew in my heart I had made room for Jesus. He was the reason I was happy. This Jesus rolled my burdens away. I felt light as I learned more about This Light.

This Jesus loved me, this I knew.

6.5 Knowing My Dad

Just as a father has compassion on his children,
So the Lord has compassion on those who fear Him.
Psalm 103:13

When I was young, I knew Mom as the one who disciplined me, took care of my basic needs, and told wonderful stories. Dad worked a lot as a postal worker, but when he was home, he was present with me.

My dad and I bonded right away from the moment he asked me to play the football game at the airport. My mom took care of me the whole day and loved me unconditionally. Somehow, however, I still had reservations with her. I was polite and obedient to my mom, but I had a hard time being freely affectionate to her. I didn't understand why until I was much older; I had a hard time with her because she was a mother figure, and I was abused by the mother of my first American family.

Over those early years, my dad became my best buddy. My dad was a big and burly man, at 6'2" and 220 lbs. He wasn't fat, but he had a round belly. He loved all kinds of sports and knew I was interested in them too. He encouraged me to try and didn't allow my handicap from polio to hinder me from playing sports. He never said anything about the way I ran. He explained the rules to basketball, football, and baseball to me. Soon I was watching the games on TV with him, whatever season it was; whether football in the fall, basketball in the winter, or baseball in the spring, we watched faithfully together. And of course, we faithfully watched the Olympics when they were aired. I just loved watching the games with him. He didn't mind me bugging him with questions. He was always so patient to discuss with me what happened in the game. He brought the love of sports out from inside of me.

Watching sports was something more than just entertainment to me. My dad explained how much work and training the athletes had to do to become who they were today. It didn't just happen. I admired these athletes. And as I grew older, I finally understood my dad's message that their success wasn't talent alone, but it was definitely this equation: Talent + Hard Work = Success.

My dad loved the great outdoors. He took me camping in the woods, and we'd spend the day fishing in the lakes or rivers. I wasn't patient enough to wait for the fish to take my bait, but I truly enjoyed spending time with him. The purpose of the camping or fishing trips wasn't for the sake of getting fish in hand. My dad wanted to spend time with me too. He wanted me to enjoy the beauty of God's creation everywhere: the sky, the woods, the body of water, the sunrise and the sunset, the sounds of birds, and the sights of other animals ⁻just going back to the simple life without TV. We always ended the camping trip with some shooting lessons. He mounted some targets on the back side of the mountain from a hundred yards, then taught me to shoot targets with a rifle. When I was able to hit them, he moved the targets a bit further. We had so much fun, and I truly enjoyed these special times with him.

My dad had amazing handyman skills. He was always repairing, whether his truck, Mom's car, or doing a house project. A lot of times he'd be under the car laying on the pavement with a piece of cardboard under his back . He also did a lot of renovations on the house as requested by Mom. He could make anything. One year, he got a Shopsmith™ Mark V Five-In-One Machine for his woodworking needs. When it came, everyone was so excited to unwrap it. This tool included a table saw, a drill press, a disk sander, horizontal boring and doweling machine, and a lathe. There was a good three-jaw chuck and key, lathe centers, extension cable, and a 10-inch combination saw blade. Also included were the legs that served as a bench and all the accessories he needed for sawing, horizontal and vertical drilling, disk sanding, and turning wood. My dad loved his new machine because it was so simple to use, yet it could handle almost any basic functions, and the results were quite nice. Moreover, the machine didn't need a great deal of space in the shop. It was around $450 for basic tools which was quite pricey, but it helped him build countless projects which saved him and Mom money in the end.

That machine really turned on his creative side. He made many beautiful wooden things from it: beautiful vases, one-piece frames for mirrors and pictures, salad bowls, lazy Susans, chess boards, and parts for renovation projects. I learned a bit about how to make bookends with him. I turned a pillar on the lathe to support books. I tinkered with the machine (with his supervision) for a while, but he could tell I wasn't interested in woodworking. I was more interested in excelling in school, sports, and playing. Maybe because of this, he never invited me to help fix things in the house or the car.

He knew I was not interested in this, so he never passed down his handyman skills to me, which to this day I regret.

Another remarkable ability of my dad's was that he had a photographic memory. He was so smart that he got a full-ride Pepsi™ scholarship for an engineering program at MIT after World War II. He forfeited that scholarship because he wanted to make money and prepare to get married. But he loved reading and never stopped learning. As a child, I saw him read all the time. He loved American history, really any history. For example, when he visited my sister in Louisiana, he had already learned the history of the battles that happened there during the Civil War. Of course, he loved to study the Bible.

On top of all these skills, my dad had such a likable personality. He was like a magnet; everybody just loved him. He always had witty jokes and made everyone chuckle. People liked being around him. He wasn't as outgoing as Mom was, but he got along with people so well. He was quite smart but was always humble and never condescending to anyone. I loved watching him interact with others. I wanted to be a polite gentleman like he was.

Now that he had me, my dad decided to start a new tradition. Every month after payday, my dad and I would drive to the one Kentucky Fried Chicken™ on the west side of town to get our monthly treat. We got a bucket of fried chicken and the trimmings, including mashed potatoes, KFC special gravy, coleslaw, and rolls. Oh, how much I looked forward to the end of the month. I loved the drumsticks so much that my dad and I made a custom. He would offer "fried chicken" at bedtime by clenching his partially hairy, index knuckle, and I would affectionately bite it and say good-night. Every night at bedtime, I asked for his special "fried chicken". I passed that tradition onto my own kids. And to this day, eating KFC drumsticks brings me such happy memories.

My dad was a man of integrity and devotion. Everyone knew and admired that about him. His faithful devotion to his responsibilities made a great impression on my life, as young as I was. He was devoted to my mom, my sisters and their families, and to me. He was loyal to his employer, the US Postal Service, and he was amazingly devoted to his God and the local church. Every Sunday, he made a commitment to take us to church, and every Sunday, we all went to church as a family.

He loved the Bible. I saw him read it every day. He also loved to teach it to other adults when he had the opportunity. He tirelessly served with various ministries and as an elder, as long as I can remember. Much later on, he got me to join the church choir with him when we had special cantata seasons.

We both sang in the bass section of our small choir when I was a teenager. Sometimes my mom also joined us in the bass section, believe it or not.

His goal was to get me into college. He felt responsible for putting me through college. He continued working until I finished college, then he retired. He joined the post office because his relatives told him it would be a good job. In the summertime, he would work at the county fair to make more money. He always got me and Mom and my sister's family tickets.

My dad was a good father and a hero to me.

6.6 Knowing My Mom

As one whom his mother comforts, so I will comfort you;
And you will be comforted in Jerusalem.
Isaiah 66:13

Although I was having reservations at being affectionate to my mom, I never doubted her love for me. I appreciated her sacrifice and the way she disciplined me. To say my mom was a spiritual giant would be true in every way. She walked by faith. She gave in faith. She wanted to make sure I grew in the Lord.

And grow in the Lord I did, because of my mom's dedication to help me in my spiritual journey. My mom's love for the Lord was so great that she understood God's heart for the lost. She was serious about winning souls for Jesus. She listened to CBN's 700 Club© (CBN Christian Broadcasting Network) and other Christian networks. She read many Christian books. She had so much fire and passion for everyone to know the Lord too. At the time, I didn't know the term for this passion or this calling to share the gospel was "evangelism," but she was certainly living her life to spread the love of Jesus with as many people as possible.

For example, during my second school year as a Pearman, my mom would drive us (me and all the many kids she babysat) after school to Good News Club. She wanted to make sure all of us would learn about the Bible. My mom didn't have to twist my arm to make me join. I loved going there. I loved the way the elderly lady, Mrs. Hart, would read us stories from the Living Bible. I really loved the way the stories came alive when she read that Bible so dramatically, like I was really there watching the story unfold. I began to wish I could have that Bible.

"Mom, I really want that Living Bible. The way Mrs. Hart told the story made me want to have that Bible with me to read anytime at home."

"Oh, that's so good for you, son! You just wait for next Wednesday. I think there is an announcement that will be exciting for you." My mom winked at me and couldn't hide her happiness.

Wednesday came, and Mrs. Hart announced that everyone who could recite the names of the books of the Old Testament correctly by memory would earn their own *The Way Living Bible*©. This was my chance; I didn't know I was an achiever, but when she said that I set my first goal in my entire life to earn that Bible.

"Genesis, Exodus, Letivi… Leviti… oh, why do the names have to be so hard?" But I had resolved in my heart to own the Bible, so I kept on practicing. After weeks and weeks of practicing, the day came when I dared to recite all the 39 challenging names of the books of the Old Testament in order by memory. After my turn, the Good News Club leader clapped and handed me my own brand-new *The Way Living Bible*©. I was thrilled to open the Bible I had earned.

My mom was so inspired that she got the church to provide Bibles for those in the Sunday school class who could recite all the books of the Bible in order. The reward was a fancy, hardback *Children's Living Bible*© with colorful pictures. Of course, I liked a friendly challenge. I earned a second Bible. To this day as an older adult, I still have that *Children's Living Bible*© at my mom's place. She asked if she could hold onto it, since she liked to read from it once in a while.

My mom was the coordinator for the Sunday School Bible challenge. She liked to add a bit more challenge and fun by asking us, "Who can spell Deuteronomy? ….. Who can spell Ecclesiastes"? Or some other difficult names of the Bible. My favorite book to spell was Ecc-les-iastes. I liked the way it rolled off the tongue so nicely. She would also have us draw our Bibles in the air by our shoulders by saying, "Draw your swords. Who can find and read Psalms 119:105?" We would all madly try to find the verse first and raise our hands. She would call on the first person to raise their hand. I really enjoyed that competition.

My mom was a bold woman! Bold— not bald; she had lots of fluffy hair. Bold. I didn't realize how bold her faith in Jesus was until I was older. I watched her go to a stranger, smiling, and introducing herself. She would say, "Hi there, how are you? My name is Clo. Do you know Jesus? Can I tell you about how wonderful Jesus is?" Just like that she would strike up a conversation and end with giving them a tract about Jesus. Anytime, anywhere and with anyone.

She was basically bold in whatever she did. If she saw any injustice— let's say someone was cutting in line—she'd firmly rebuke that person. She would say, "Excuse me, young man, I think that lady was in front of you, so she should be served first." Or, if someone was rude to her parents, she'd remark,

101

"I'm sorry, young lady, I don't want to intrude, but the way you treat your mom isn't the best, and you know it."

But most of her conversations would be to tell people about Jesus. She found inventive ways for creative evangelism. She'd put a few dollars and a Christian tract under the bill when we ate out so that the waitress would find it and read it. She'd put dollar bills and tracts in restrooms, inside the phone booth coin spaces, and inside the yellow phone book in the phone booth. I would see Mom crisscrossing the mall and gleefully putting tracts in various strategic places. If she saw a homeless person in front of a store or a restaurant, she'd buy food, and then put a few dollar bills and a tract inside the bag and give it to the person. It had become expected wherever we went—the post office, the bank, the park, the library, anywhere she'd talk to strangers—and then give out tracts and offer some dollars. At that awkward age, I felt very uncomfortable when she went out of her way to share what Jesus had done in her life. I would try to look the other way or walk a bit away from her. I wondered, *what if they got offended?* But my mom always shared with great compassion and love.

She also started a "penny ministry." Wherever she saw pennies on the ground, she would bring them home and drop them in a jar. When she had the jar full, Dad and I would roll them up in penny-roller cylinders. We had fun rolling those pennies up to see how many pennies there were in each collection. Mom then would deposit them at the bank and right away write a check to send to the ministry that printed tracts in other languages. My mom was a missionary from home to other countries. She even persuaded her local church to deposit loose change into a big jar for the "penny ministry." Only God knows how many people got to know Jesus with her "little" ministry.

I truly never met anyone else that bold, passionate, creative, and enthusiastic in sharing the gospel. I really had a lot to learn from Mom.

CHAPTER

07

Elementary School Years

The mind of the prudent acquires knowledge,
And the ear of the wise seeks knowledge.

Proverbs 18:15

7.1. School Life in the '70s

Acquire wisdom! Acquire understanding! Do not forget nor turn away from the words of my mouth. Do not forsake her, and she will guard you; Love her, and she will watch over you.
Proverbs 4: 5-6

In school in the 1970s, we had no computers nor even hand-held calculators. They existed already but were too expensive for everyone to buy. We learned mostly by listening attentively to our teachers, and we did all our work in our notebooks. We went to the library to check out paper-bound books to read and for our research. We used a dictionary to learn the meanings of words we didn't know. We had homeroom teachers who taught most of the subjects except for physical education, music and band. We addressed our teachers by "Mr." and "Ms." or "Mrs." and their family names. We started each day with the *Pledge of Allegiance*. We had a lot of fun studying, playing, and eating together. We didn't have much bullying and I was not treated differently although I was the only Asian kid in the whole school.

At Riverside Elementary School, I had Mrs. Dorothy Wilson for second grade, Mrs. Jane Smith for third grade, Mrs. Schuchard for fourth grade, Mrs. Muckey for fifth grade, Mr. Magnussen (the PE coach), and Mr. Richard Bagley for sixth grade. They were all very kind and dedicated. All of these teachers focused on the basics of education called the 3Rs: Reading, 'Riting (writing), and 'Rithmetic (arithmetic). Every day we had reading sessions which covered comprehension, oral reading, and word attack skills. In oral reading, we practiced reading smoothly. Word attack skills included spelling and learning new words using a dictionary. Even though I was from Korea, I was able to learn phonics skills quite fast by sounding out the individual letters, blends, and combinations, all without any accent by this time. Spelling was fun and challenging for me.

Writing skills included learning to write in complete sentences, writing an original story in paragraph form, using correct grammar and correct mechanics of punctuation and capitalization. This was harder for me since I was a perfectionist. I wanted every sentence to be perfect, so I kept erasing and needed more time than my friends did. In fourth grade, we started writing lots of book reports, and I had to persevere through each one.

We had to learn how to write longhand (cursive), and I received so much praise, both from my teachers and my parents for my neat and beautiful penmanship.

Soon I forgot Hangul, the Korean alphabet and writing system that I learned in the Korean schools. The Hangul writing system has a letter order or a stroke order, just like Chinese and Japanese writings, but I liked the English alphabet writing system. It was less complicated, and you could make the letters pretty by making thin and thick strokes, not so rigid like the Korean Hangul. I found practicing penmanship so fun and relaxing.

It was fortunate that my schooling in Korea gave me a head start in math. In fourth grade, my peers were still learning addition, subtraction, multiplication, division, and word problems, which I had mastered in second grade in Korea. I was always ahead in math and accurate in calculating. This gave me confidence in math skills and in sciences classes later on. I enjoyed doing experiments and observing the scientific process that took place. And for the first time, writing the science report was fun because I used my critical analysis and reference skills from the observation instead of the boring book reports.

Interestingly, I found myself being keen at social studies, especially reading history. It was almost like I wanted to know all about American history to catch up on my new identity. I felt that in order to be completely immersed and assimilated as an American boy going to school with all these white American kids, I needed to forget and release my own Korean history. I still wanted to bury that part of me deep inside my soul to the point that I would forget it forever.

I thought this immersion, this assimilation, was my way of being *born again*. I didn't realize this was my winning formula coming out, trying to solve problems by forgetting everything about my past instead of asking Jesus to be my solution, my true winning formula.

7.2. Back to School Routine

Do not store up for yourselves treasures on earth, where moth and rust destroy, and where thieves break in and steal. But store up for yourselves treasures in heaven, where neither moth nor rust destroys, and where thieves do not break in or steal; for where your treasure is, there your heart will be also.
Matthew 6: 19-21

"No, David, we are not getting those Levi's™ jeans. These ones will do," my mom said again, and her voice was getting impatient. I sighed and knew this was a battle I could never win.

People said, "never say never," but what if I had to say it? Back-to-school shopping for clothes was *never* fun for me. My mom always took me to Montgomery Ward™, a retail shopping store that was famous back in the '70s, when the big box stores were beginning to open. Ward's would send seasonal catalogs, and I'd devour the toy pages, especially the Christmas edition. I loved looking at race cars, electric trains, and other toys they featured. So, I had a lot of hopes going to Ward's with my mom. Soon we all called it "Monkey Ward's," but when I went shopping, I was disappointed because the experience wasn't what I expected from looking at the alluring catalogs.

"So, David, I'm getting these for you, okay?" My mom broke my thoughts.

"Okay, sure, Mom." I knew I had to be thankful, although I didn't like the no-brand jeans. My friends talked about their Levi's™ jeans. They did look cool on them, but I knew they were too expensive for us. They also had nice, brand name shoes, but my mom insisted on the plain, old canvas shoes for me. I just went with the flow and wanted the shopping to be over. This happened year after year.

Mom went ahead and picked out some new t-shirts for me and proceeded to the cashier. I followed closely, and now I could smile, because now the fun part could start. I didn't like shopping for clothes, but stationery was my favorite.

We stopped at another store to get stationery. She asked me to pick out a lunch box. I quickly chose a boy theme because I didn't care about this part. Then she grabbed five composition books (one each for reading, writing, science, social science, and one extra). She grabbed a box of pencils with erasers on their tops, a long ruler, two pens of black and blue, a pack of 12 color-crayons, a set of 12 color-markers, and a set of colored papers for my art class. She was so fast at picking these items, as if she was already equipped with a list from our homeroom teacher. Maybe she knew if it were up to me, I would take much longer trying to decide which pens I liked, and which crayon set to get. I probably would like to try each marker to make sure each worked properly. So, before I knew it, she was already heading to the cashier to pay.

Next, we went to the grocery store. There we got four loaves of bread, a jar of peanut butter, a jar of strawberry jam, a jar of mustard, a jar of mayonnaise, a pack of bologna, a pack of American cheese slices, a jug of whole milk, a pint of chocolate milk, a box of powdered drink mix, several cans of tuna fish in oil, a jar of sandwich spread, some apples and, last but not least, a box of Twinkies™.

At home, she put all the new clothes in the wash. Then she put out all the stationery and told me to write my name on each item. After that, she opened the grocery bags and showed me how to pack my lunch. She said I should prepare that ahead of time so I wouldn't rush before the bus picked me up in the morning. I had cafeteria food on certain days, but on other days I brought a sack lunch.

"So, David, if you want to make a bologna sandwich then all you need to do is first spread yellow mustard or some mayonnaise on one side of the bread. Then put the bologna on top of it. Unwrap a slice of cheese and put it on top of the bologna. Put another piece of bread on top of it to make a sandwich and cut the sandwich in half. Then wrap the sandwich in cling wrap and put it in your lunch box. Do you get this?"

"Yes, Mom. I made it before."

"OK, great!"

But I usually made my favorite peanut butter and strawberry jam sandwich. I liked to toast the sandwich first. Sometimes I alternated it with grape jelly. Only a few times did I bring a bologna sandwich with mayonnaise to school.

When my mom prepared meals from canned tuna fish, I took the leftover and mixed it with sandwich spread to make a tuna fish sandwich for lunch, but I never brought it to school with the fear that it would make my breath stink.

I enjoyed having Twinkies™ at school! It was such a treat for me, and I always shared it with a friend. But they soon ran out, and my mom didn't always buy more afterwards.

On hot afternoons after playing, I made drinks by mixing one envelope of drink mix with cold water and ice. I liked it but didn't like the part where the color stained my tongue for the whole day.

I was glad my mom taught me to be frugal. I learned not to be materialistic, not to value items more than people, since things wouldn't last anyway. My friends' brand name jeans were good, but soon they would be too small on them. Their brand name shoes would soon show their wear and tear. My mom taught me that although she saved on those items, she was generous in giving and sharing her resources with the lost and the poor, which had more eternal value than buying things. Although I was embarrassed and sometimes resentful that I didn't always have nice things, deep inside I knew that my mom treasured something that moths and rust couldn't destroy. She really walked the talk.

7.3 Discovering New Talents

Delight yourself in the Lord;
And He will give you the desires of your heart.
Psalm 37:4

The rest of my elementary years, in my opinion, were flying by too fast. My friends were basically the same friends from fourth grade through sixth grade. My parents decided that I should stay with the same friends I had made in the fourth grade rather than moving me up. Since I was advanced in certain subjects like math and English (for some reason), I would attend those periods with the fifth graders, and I did the same when I advanced to fifth-grade. It was nice to have friends from the same grade and from one grade above. We heard stories of the dreaded rod of Mr. Gordon, who used his rod to discipline his students when needed. If you didn't behave, you'd get whipped. None of us wanted to be in his class. Thankfully, I was spared. I had Mrs. Muckey instead.

My dad always told me that the physical effects of polio should not be an excuse for me not to not try something. He said if I couldn't run as well as others, then I could compensate in another way. I liked to play, so I was always with my athletic friends. They found out that I was quite athletic, even with my leg. My hand and eye coordination were very good. We always played sports together during recess. I discovered that I was good at throwing and pitching a baseball.

One day we were together, and the sixth-grade girls were passing by. We boys started challenging them saying, "We can beat you girls!" The sixth-grade girls were already big and tall. We boys were still in fourth grade and puny compared to them. Soon we heard the captain of the girls say, "Okay, if you can beat us, which we doubt you can, we will treat you to ice cream cones, but if we win, you will treat us."

So one afternoon, we had a friendly baseball game with the girls. They were quite good athletes. I was made a pitcher by my friends. It was a tough game, but we won. We got a little cocky for beating them.

Mainly, I was very happy that my dad was right. Having polio shouldn't be an excuse for me to not play sports, but it should be a motivation to work harder, more creatively, and to be better. I came home and told my dad about our win. He was pleased for the most part, except for the cockiness in my story. I wasn't sure if we all demanded that ice cream cone or not from the girls. Maybe we didn't.

It was also in the sixth grade that I had a memorable event which led me to discover my gymnastics talent. On a Friday afternoon, Mr. Magnussen, the custodian and the PE teacher, announced that he planned to start a gymnastics club. Although I was chosen as a pitcher for baseball by my friends, I was always afraid to try out for formal sports teams at school. The main reason was because I was self-conscious of my awkward, skinny left leg. I loved most sports, especially basketball, but back then the basketball trunks were so short, and my left leg would be revealed to the world. The baseball team I joined with my friends was informal and just for fun, so I could wear my sweatpants when playing. But sports teams had uniforms, and I didn't want my left leg to show. So, I didn't plan to try out.

Mr. Magnusson approached me to talk about joining gymnastics.

"David, I think you'd really be good at this. You have strong arms and great coordination. I think you should try it before saying 'no.'"

He could tell I was restless, but how could I possibly share the real reason? It seemed so lame. I was quiet for a while, looking for words.

But somehow, he got it.

"David, you could just wear long sweatpants. I know running would be hard for you. So, you won't need to do the floor exercise and the pommel horse as they require running, jumping, and leg control."

"So, what is left for me to do, Mr. Magnussen? I don't understand."

He gave me a fatherly smile as he showed me a special apparatus for gymnastics called climbing ropes. He challenged me, saying, "David, during the performance, if you can climb the rope without using your legs, I will buy you an ice-cream cone." I shook hands with him. The rest was history.

Right there my next special talent was born. I took his challenge and practiced hard every day. Soon I did what nobody else in the school could do: I could climb the rope up to the ceiling rafters without using my feet. I broke the good news to my parents that I had been chosen to join the formal gymnastics team of our school. My parents were so proud and happy. When I looked at my dad, I could see twinkling in his eyes. He knew how much that meant to me.

We performed before our entire school assembly. My friends performed gymnastic moves on the pommel horse, did acrobatic flips, and walked across

110

the gym floor on their hands to the applause of the entire assembly. Then the spotlight came to me. It was my turn to climb the rope. After Mr. Magnusson introduced the feat I would attempt, I came to center stage on the floor below the 30 feet rope that was dangling from the rafters. I was nervous, but I knew I could do it. I swiftly ascended the rope with ease and slammed the rafter at the rousing applause and cheers from the assembly, and then I descended to the wooden floor like some sort of kung-fu disciple.

Everybody applauded my accomplishment enthusiastically. I enjoyed the attention, but most of all I enjoyed the vanilla ice-cream cone that Mr. Magnusson bought me.

The gymnastic event was so popular that we were invited to perform at all the Roseburg elementary schools. I found out later that all the other schools' ceilings were shorter than ours since Riverside's gymnasium was originally built for a junior high school. So yes, it was a bit easier to perform my event, but Mr. Magnusson still bought me an ice-cream cone every time I accomplished my feat. Then the gymnastic season was over, and so was my sixth-grade year.

One night at dinner, my mom reflected on how good God was to allow me to discover two new talents in the area of sports, since I always desired this in my heart but was too shy to mention it out loud. She quoted Psalm 37:4 to me, "Delight yourself in the Lord, and He will give you the desires of your heart."

Then she said, "Well, David, the Lord has seen how much you have delighted in going to Good News Club every Wednesday and in memorizing the Bible because you want more of Him, so He did give you the desires of your heart. You didn't have to say it to anyone, but He knew how much you wanted to be able to play sports. So, he gave you a favor to play baseball as a pitcher with your friends and to join this gymnastics team at school and even to perform. So, the way I see it, Psalm 37:4 did happen to you because God sees everything, and He is a good God."

111

7.4 Finishing Strong

The end of a matter is better than its beginning;
Patience of spirit is better than haughtiness of spirit.
Ecclesiastes 7: 8

The year 1976 was very special for our country since it was the celebration of the 200th Anniversary of our Independence. So, the United States celebrated all year long. For our school, we celebrated in the spring, although Independence Day wasn't until July 4th. I was part of the school choir which sang patriotic songs to our hearts desire. We didn't sing just to our assembly, but on the television in our community. I really enjoyed singing patriotic songs; they made me feel more American than ever. I was very proud and privileged.

At the end of school, we always came together for a final assembly where special awards were announced. The one award that ended the assembly was always the "Student of the Year Award." The year before, my friend Scott from grade 6 received the award. I had always worked hard because that work ethic was planted in me since I was in foster homes and in the orphanage. That was my winning formula to survive. I should never make trouble, and working hard was one of the ways not to make trouble.

I wondered if I would ever be a candidate for that award. I had a slight inclination of that possibility, but I brushed it off as only a wish and not even a realistic goal of mine.

In the assembly, before announcing the award, Mr. Crane, our principal, stated there would be two deserving students. He then declared, "The first recipient for the Student of the Year Award is given to David Pearman!" My heart beat heavily, my eyes became bright, and my face became rose-red as I excitedly went down from the bleachers to receive the award with a sheepish smile. My friend Phillip also received the award. We both were so elated and congratulated each other.

From the stage, I looked for Mrs. Wilson, Mrs. Smith, Mrs. Schuchard, Mrs. Muckey, Mr. Magnussen, and Mr. Bagley. They were in a row of teachers, sitting together. They nodded at me and I smiled at them, knowing that I couldn't have done this without their patience and perseverance. They helped me overcome my English barriers in my early years and believed that I could succeed. This award was as much for them as it was for me.

Mr. Crane asked if I wanted to say something. I was too shy to say anything, but I lifted the award and nodded to all my teachers and friends to show my gratitude.

CHAPTER

08

The Shepherding of My Heart

What man among you, if he has a hundred sheep and has lost one of them, does not leave the ninety-nine in the open pasture and go after the one which is lost until he finds it? When he has found it, he lays it on his shoulders, rejoicing. And when he comes home, he calls together his friends and his neighbors, saying to them, 'Rejoice with me, for I have found my sheep which was lost!' I tell you that in the same way, there will be more joy in heaven over one sinner who repents than over ninety-nine righteous persons who need no repentance.
Luke 15: 4-7

8.1 The Shepherd and the Lamb

I myself will be the shepherd of my sheep, and I myself will make them lie down, declares the Lord God. I will seek the lost, and I will bring back the strayed, and I will bind up the injured, and I will strengthen the weak.
Ezekiel 34: 15-16 ESV

One of the passages I memorized in my Wednesday Good News Club was from Psalm 23. I had heard my Bible teacher, Mrs. Hart, talk a few times about Jesus as the Good Shepherd. On one of the living room walls, my mom also had a painting of Jesus with a shepherd's staff guiding and protecting the sheep. Still, I didn't understand what it fully meant, especially about me being a sheep and Jesus being a shepherd. Then an incident happened that gave me a picture of this relationship between a sheep and a shepherd.

In all my years of being a student at Riverside Elementary School, there was one person I never really got to know. That person was Mr. Roy Crane, the principal. One afternoon, as my friends and I were running and laughing to catch the bus home, I ran my right knee into a red-brick, landscaped wall that protruded out from the classroom. My right knee was my good knee, so I lost my balance and fell to the ground. The pain overtook me, and it was so intense that I couldn't help but cry. As I was bawling my eyes out, Mr. Crane came out from his office and tended to my injury. He asked me if I had pain with movement. He checked to see if my knee was tender. He asked if I was able to stand or walk, and if I could straighten out my leg.

He shouted to his secretary to get some ice packs, and as soon as they were in his hands, he applied them on my injured knee. He was so calm the whole time that I can't remember when I stopped crying. Then he told me he was going to carry me to the car, so he directed where I should put both my hands to make it easier for him to carry me. He then carried me to the passenger's seat and drove me home in his car.

When we got home, he carried me all the way to the living room and set me on the couch. He talked to my mom about what happened and how I needed to rest my knee for a while, keep the ice packs on it every 15 minutes for two hours, and elevate my leg for the rest of the day. He joked with my mom that he learned that from having four boys himself. As he was talking to my mom in the living room, my eyes looked back and forth between him and my mom. They were sitting facing each other. Above the loveseat where Mr. Crane was sitting, hung the picture of Jesus guiding the lamb. It then dawned on me that Mr. Crane was like Jesus as the shepherd, and I was like the lamb. He had attended to my injury so carefully like Jesus tended the lamb.

The next day I was famous among my friends because my injury was so special that the most important man in the school, the principal himself, carried me home. I enjoyed that attention, but more important, God used that incident to teach me about the special relationship between the Shepherd and the lamb.

8.2 The Most Important Decision

For you were continually straying like sheep, but now you have returned to the Shepherd and Guardian of your souls.
1 Peter 2: 25

During my grammar school years, another special person God brought into my life was Pastor Dick Halaas at Westside Christian Church. Pastor Dick really had a shepherding heart. God had given him such a huge heart to love people. He prioritized people. He wanted to know how everyone was doing in their job, their marriage, parenting, in relationships, and in life. He didn't want people to come just to hear him preach. He wanted to know them, and for them to get to know him too.

Pastor Dick wanted to know me personally. He was God's instrument of encouragement in my life. He showed compassion and empathy early on when he learned my adoption story from my mom, but he advised wisely, "David, for all your trials and troubles God has given you supernatural strength to endure, so never allow self-pity to rise in your heart. That is the work of the devil. Remember greater is He that is within you than he that is in the world."

That message stuck with me. When he encouraged me to go to summer youth camp, I went. When he vouched for me to play sports with the church softball team, I played, even with my physical challenges. He never stopped encouraging me in my walk with the Lord to become a more mature person. Beyond that, he influenced me in making the most important decision of my life.

During my sixth-grade year on Mother's Day at church, the most important decision of my life was posed to me. Every Sunday, Pastor Dick would end his sermon by inviting people to make a decision to follow Jesus as the Savior and Lord of their lives. Every week he did that, and every week my gut had an uneasy feeling. I wanted to accept the invitation, but something was stopping me. I was too shy to stand in front of everyone.

This Mother's Day, Pastor Dick purposely shortened his sermon. He knew there were a lot of guests coming to church, just like for Christmas and Easter. Some husbands and fathers (who were usually at home, letting the

118

women and children come to church by themselves) were in attendance. At the end of the sermon, as the pianist played *Just As I Am©*, he invited as usual, "If you are here today and you've never believed in Jesus for the forgiveness of your sins, come to the front. I am going to pray a prayer of salvation so you can pray along with me and receive that free gift that Jesus has offered you by believing in your heart." I was restless, but I wasn't sure if I should go to the altar. I felt I had believed in Jesus, but I just never confessed it. I felt my hands suddenly become clammy. Besides, going to the front seemed so scary for me.

Then Pastor Dick continued, "Also, you might be here today, and you remember you have believed in Jesus in the past, but over a period of time you've become distant from God. Maybe you keep a sin in your life and think God is upset with you. God is here welcoming you back. If you'd like to recommit yourself to Him today, you can pray the same prayer along with me." My heart beat faster and my hands felt clammier. I wanted to come forward but still something stopped me. I felt I knew Jesus a lot from my family and my Good News Bible Club, but I just never said the prayer. What to do? And still, going to the front and being watched by all the people in the pews was adding to the tension.

A second later, Pastor Dick's voice gently pleaded, "Maybe you are here, and you've been in church for years but don't know that you know; you know that you know you are saved. It's okay, just pray along with me too and receive that assurance in Jesus." My heart exclaimed, *That's me! I believe in Jesus! I just wanted to be sure!* But my feet felt heavy to take the first step to get out of the pew and to go to the front.

At the same time, my dad looked at me knowing I was struggling to make a decision. So, he pressed my clammy hands and whispered gently, "Do you want me to walk with you to the front?" I nodded my head "yes", and we walked hand-in-hand to the front of the church.

Pastor Dick smiled and said, "It's been a long time coming, David."

That day I invited Jesus to be my Lord and Savior in front of the church assembly. I was baptized under the water the following Tuesday evening in the presence of my parents and a few friends. I didn't have a spiritual surge of emotions, but I knew I had made the right decision. I did not know at that time that my decision would carry me through the ups and downs of my life. I started to understand about Jesus being the Shepherd of my soul. The following years, Jesus would patiently show me that He wanted to be my *winning* formula, and not the ones I had made up to survive with my own strength.

8.3 I Shall Not Want

The Lord is my shepherd, I shall not want.
Psalm 23: 1

"David, what do you think about taking care of Kevin and Greg this summer?" Mom asked while I was washing dishes one pleasant evening in May.

"How come you're not doing it, Mom?" I inquired.

"Well, since it's summer break, the kids won't have school, so Mrs. Rasmunsen thought it would be a great idea to have them stay at their own house. I can't come to their house every day. I have to take care of the other kids here," Mom explained.

"Ok, Mom. I'll think about it." I replied.

Mom had given me odd jobs like vacuuming or mowing the lawn once in a while and awarded me with some spending money after the task was completed. I enjoyed making a little money. Combining my birthday money with what I earned, I was able to buy birthday gifts for my parents, a few baseball cards, and pens. That felt good.

So, I accepted the offer. That summer would be my first time working at an actual job. Every day I would ride my bike up the big Brooklyn Avenue then turn off to the right to Winter Street. Then came the hardest part: Winter Street rose straight up, a very steep hill, and I could feel the burn in my thigh muscles as I rode up. After one miserable week, going up that street was a piece of cake. My muscles were trained and didn't complain anymore.

I took the job not thinking too much about the challenges of the job. I was glad it went smoothly. Kevin and Greg liked me, and I made some money. I worked for two and a half months (half of June, all of July, and all of August). At the end of each day, I put an "X" on the calendar to keep track of my days. I never had a sick day. In total, I made quite a sum of money. I had never made that much in my life, and the job just suddenly fell into my lap. I was glad I made the decision not to have the money every Friday, because I would not have accumulated that whole amount. I would have splurged some of my pay every weekend.

I shared that excitement with my dad. That was when I learned the concept of tithing. My dad told me how God really meant it when He says in Psalm 23:1, *"The Lord is my shepherd; I shall not want."*

Dad said, "David, this is a testimony of God in your life that when you made the Lord your Shepherd, then He'd make sure you always have all you need. You shall not be in want. The job fell suddenly into your lap because He wanted to bless you and show you He is your Provider. He'll continue to make Himself faithful as your Shepherd and Provider. You are His sheep. Remember that."

Dad continued, "Now the Bible also teaches us to be thankful and not to be attached to money. One way to do that is by giving Him back our tithe and offering. Tithe is 10% of our earnings. When you do that, it blesses the church, and the Lord promises that He will rebuke the devourer that tries to steal, kill, and destroy your harvest."

I cheerfully tithed my 10% the following Sunday. I felt so grown up.

This would begin my pattern of getting a job from sixth grade through high school. Someone would offer me a job, and I obliged and took the job. People we knew would offer me jobs, like cleaning the doctor's office on Saturdays, sweeping the downtown department store after school, and working as a service man at a gas station over the summer. During those years, I never looked for a job. I believe these were God's provisions without me even asking for them.

The Lord truly showed not only that He was the Shepherd of my soul, but also the Shepherd of my provisions too.

CHAPTER

09

The Teen Years

But you are a chosen race, a royal priesthood, a holy nation, a people for God's own possession, so that you may proclaim the excellencies of Him who has called you out of darkness into His marvelous light;
1 Peter 2:9

9.1 Facing My Fear

But if any of you lacks wisdom, let him ask of God, who gives to all generously and without reproach, and it will be given to him.
James 1:5

Being a teen is a challenging time for most people, and it certainly was for me. It wasn't just the awkwardness and the confusion of managing the various changes that happened all at once - like the physical changes in my body and the emotional changes that put me on a roller coaster all the time. It was also the unfamiliar feeling that my brain was in a different mode where I wasn't accessing my logic and critical reasoning or good judgment as easily as before. My teachers and counselors never talked about these crazy changes (except the biological changes), and I was too shy to ask my parents. As a result, my way of solving problems was by overthinking everything and going into either fight, flight, or freeze mode, depending on what was coming my way.

That summer after sixth grade, I joined Summer Kids Camp at Little River Christian Camp. I asked my mom if she could cover for me for a week of my kid-sitting job. I actually didn't want to go, but good old Pastor Dick promoted it so much that I changed my mind. I went with reservations in my heart.

The camp was located in a beautiful, mountain town called Glide, Oregon. It was resting on 15 acres of forest land in the middle of the Umpqua National Forest along Little River. The camp crew was ready for us. When we arrived, we were greeted by friendly adults and the smell of hotdogs being prepared for us.

The Camp Leaders took us to our cabins. We were put in different groups for cabin arrangement and the duties schedule. We all were so excited to explore the beautiful forest and the river. It was definitely going to be a wonderful camp adventure full of games and fun.

I loved our boys' cabin. It had four bunk beds in each room and four cabinets to put our bags in. I liked all my roommates, including Paul, Samuel, and Dan. The four of us all had Bible names! So, when we were asked to name our group, we named it: the Bible Heroes. We made Paul our group leader.

When we all checked out the bathroom and where we had to shower, I froze. There were toilet stalls, but there was only one open shower room. There were 10 showers but no curtains dividing them. I decided right then and there to evade showering the whole time I was at camp. Yes, I was not going to risk my dignity in front of others.

We heard the bell from the main hall which was the sign for assembly. The camp leader explained the schedule:

Breakfast was from 7:30 - 8:30 am at the dining hall (If you were the breakfast crew, then you had to get ready earlier and be at the kitchen at 7am. If you were the cleaning crew, you would help clean from 8-9am). We all started to eat together after the morning prayer.

Morning sessions would start at 9am. There were usually three sessions: that consisted of singing and Bible study in the big room, an activity (like crafts, drama, or games), then a break. After that, we would do some kind of sports (like swimming, ping-pong, basketball, 500 baseball, box hockey, Frisbee, or some other kind of physical activity). Then it was lunch time. Again, different groups were responsible for preparation and for cleaning.

After lunch, we had "quiet time" when we had to go to our cabin, read a devotion, and write a reflection in the workbook. If we wanted to, we were allowed to take a nap or go play. Some girls wrote in each other's notebooks and talked and giggled. I did my devotional really fast so I could use the rest of my time playing in the big field. I didn't like to explore so much. I liked walking, but too much walking caused my feet to be sore.

When the quiet time was over, we went back to the dining hall. The camp leaders gave us two tickets so we could choose two treats each afternoon. I liked all their snacks.

I thought Paul, Sam, and Dan looked so fresh from swimming or taking a shower. I didn't want to shower with them, and I would certainly not go swimming. I knew how to swim, but I didn't want to put on my swimming trunks to show my legs.

After snacks we had some free time, but we had to use it to prepare some kind of talent show with our group. We would have to perform on the last night of camp, and there would be a prize for the winner. I was glad my group decided to do a simple drama with a bit of singing. I heard Nathan's group was going to dance. Joanna Miller was a dancer, and she was going to choreograph it. I wasn't sure I would do a good job on that, and I certainly didn't want to let my group down. I could do a little drama and singing but not dancing, and definitely not in front of Joanna.

We headed for dinner at the dining hall, and then it was the best time of all when we all gathered around the bonfire. If you looked up, you could see the starry night inside the circle of tall pine trees. We sang songs, some people shared, and then a guest speaker or the pastor preached and concluded with a sweet prayer time and more songs. We usually ended with singing one of my favorites, *Pass It On©*; it was both inspirational and romantic.

I loved our first day, but still I couldn't enjoy it fully since the dread of showering continued to occupy my mind. I tried to keep clean by washing my face and arms really well several times a day.

The next day, we all woke up and got ready. I went to the bathroom to brush my teeth and wash my face. I saw some kids decided to take a shower and some who went for a swim yesterday didn't. I sneakily went with the ones who didn't shower, although I didn't swim either. I thought, *who would have known?* Every day there were two different groups: the ones who showered in the morning and the ones who showered after swimming. I thought people would assume I either showered in the morning or in the afternoon after swimming. All I needed to do was to keep myself from being too sweaty so I wouldn't smell since this camp was a week long.

To my dismay, the camp leaders really got us sweaty each day. They had prepared a treasure hunt game for our groups. I felt like they hid them too well in the 15 acres of the forest. Actually, they hid them only in the main areas, but the places were too tricky, like inside a hollow tree or under a loose brick. Finally, after we all scoured different trails, we managed to get 18 items out of 20 in the list and won second prize. That was great because we didn't win the talent show.

Even with the hot and sweaty days, I was resolute about evading showers creatively. After the last session one day Paul suggested, "We're all so stinky. Let's shower and then get our snacks early." Everyone agreed but I mumbled, "Oh, I have a tummy ache. I'll just shower later. You guys go ahead." Then I ran to one of the bathroom stalls and waited there.

After four days of not taking a shower, Pastor Dick somehow found out I didn't shower. I got caught. I told him I was too bashful to shower in an open shower area for boys. Fortunately, he just shook his head.

"David, you have to face your fear. Why don't you take a shower right now? It's really not healthy to miss a shower for this many days."

I was embarrassed by his reprimand, so I did it. I took a really fast shower, so I wasn't super clean, but at least I got water from the top of my head to the tip of my toes. I didn't realize how much I let this shower struggle take over the fun part of camp.

When I got home, I thought, *oh wow. I could have taken a shower very early in the morning before anyone woke up or late at night when everyone was getting ready to sleep.* Like I said, that was the time when my emotions took over my logic and critical reasoning that I used to depend on. And I had forgotten to ask God for wisdom to solve my shower problem.

9.2. Puppy Love

Therefore, accept one another, just as Christ also accepted us to the glory of God.
Romans 15: 7

Another change I experienced was infatuations over girls. In fact, it seemed I had a crush on a new girl every few months, even as early as the sixth grade. I didn't make any moves, since I was too shy to say anything to them, let alone approach them. These were girls at school or at church. My friends would tease me like crazy if they found out.

But something happened one year at Little River Christian Camp. I found Joanna Miller to be so attractive. I liked the way she was so kind to everyone. I thought her smile was so pretty and her laugh so contagious. Moreover, she was a bit sporty too. Then I watched her help Nathan's group with the dance talent show, and I was smitten. Joanna was a girl from Sutherlin, the next town north of Roseburg. The surprising thing was she seemed to like me, but how would I know for sure? She seemed friendly to everyone.

The answer came soon enough. My friend Paul confirmed it when we were cleaning dishes alone. Sam and Dan were getting dirty plates from the tables, so they didn't hear our conversation.

"Why are you smiling alone like a crazy person?" Paul suddenly interrupted my thoughts.

"What do you mean? I wasn't smiling." I denied it.

"You definitely were. And I asked you for a rag earlier, but you didn't hear me because you were thinking about that girl."

"What girl? I wasn't thinking about any girl." My voice went up to cover my embarrassment.

"You know, David, I think Joanna Miller likes you.?" Paul kept teasing me.

"What do you mean?"

"You want to know how I know? She's been wearing your baseball cap around the camp."

Joanna had wanted to wear my North Eugene High School baseball cap. I was surprised she suddenly grabbed it from me one time, so I let her borrow it for the rest of the camp. It was a special cap since the NBA superstar Danny Ainge graduated from that school. I was flattered that she kept wearing it.

"Oh, that was because it was so hot during the 500 baseball challenge and she didn't bring her hat," I tried to reason, but I was so happy Paul noticed that I wanted to jump up and down.

"You have to believe me, David, because I have two big brothers to learn from and you don't. They talk about this all the time. In high school, if a girl proudly wears a boy's letterman jacket that means she is going steady with him. So, Joanna is hinting that she likes you."

So that settled it. Paul's advice boosted extra boldness in me.

I quickly made a plan.

We were going to have a special banquet at the end of the week on Friday night after the talent show. It would be our last night. The camp leader had said that after the talent show, we wouldn't need to sit with our groups anymore so we could sit anywhere at the big banquet tables.

I wanted to invite Joanna to sit with me at the banquet, but I was worried I would get tongue-tied when I saw her face-to-face. So, at night I tore a blank page from my camp notebook and wrote Joanna a neat letter.

Hi Joanna!

I was wondering if we could sit together for the special banquet since we wouldn't need to sit with our groups. I have a card trick I want to show you.

Then I signed my name. I couldn't sleep that night thinking about the plan.

I gave it to her in the morning at breakfast. She read it quickly and nodded shyly with the prettiest smile.

That Friday I wore my denim, long-sleeve cowboy shirt with silvery studded buttons. Studded buttons were in fashion at that time. My sister gave me the shirt for my birthday just before I went to camp. I was glad I brought that. I was also secretly grateful Pastor Dick forced me to shower on Thursday.

Joanna wore a white blouse paired with a pullover denim vest and a long, pleated denim skirt. She also put a white ribbon in her hair. It was funny that we wore somewhat matching clothes.

Paul saw us and winked at me. It was official, my first puppy love relationship.

After camp, Joanna and I wrote letters back and forth. I called her a few times, but we never met. Calling was hard enough for me, since I had to do it in the kitchen where the phone was, and I was afraid my mom or dad would hear me talk.

We lived far enough apart that we didn't dare ask our parents to take us to meet. I was too shy to ask my parents to take me to her house, and what would her parents think about me visiting? And I didn't want to bother my parents with my silly puppy love story anyway. Oh, how I wished we were attending the same church; it would make my life much easier. But she went to First Christian Church in Roseburg which was closer than Sutherlin, and I went to Westside. So how could we meet?

It was too much to think about as young kids. After a few months, our letters stopped, and we never met again. Joanna never returned to camp, so I never saw her again.

All in all, I had no regrets. My puppy love relationship with Joanna gave me the nice and warm feeling of being accepted and wanted in a relationship. I continued to have crushes on girls, but I didn't have another "romantic" relationship until high school.

9.3 Growing as a Youth

Let no one look down on your youthfulness, but rather in speech, conduct, love, faith and purity, show yourself an example of those who believe.
1 Timothy 4:12

Adolescence is a meandering journey, and my youth pastor, Pastor Stan Wesolowski, perceived the complexity it carried. Although we were anchored in our Christian faith, he saw how we could easily drift amidst the pressures and uncertainties of teen life.

Upon reflecting on Pastor Stan's vision for us, I remember a particular conversation that shaped our youth gatherings. "Our inner struggles, like feelings of inferiority and all kinds of temptations (sexually and anything related to integrity), are battles worth fighting," he shared one evening. "How we navigate through these challenges, uphold integrity, and embrace leadership forms the pillars of our personal and spiritual growth."

In deciphering the myriad of questions that sprouted during adolescence about our identity and purpose, he gave us the space to explore and understand our faith personally.

One day, I asked him, "How can we know our faith is ours, not just an echo of our parents' beliefs?"

With a thoughtful nod, he replied, "It begins with questions just like that one. Pursuing understanding, asking why, and seeking God in your unique way will carve out a path that is unmistakably yours."

Engaging with our peers was a pivotal part of our journey. Pastor Stan once said, "We need our ministry, one where we not only come for ourselves but also reach out to others with open arms and hearts." The next thing we knew, we were making "HOT" and "COLD" lists as a heartfelt plea to extend our youth community's warmth and love to others.

We learned quickly that designing youth church services required a blend of strategic planning and a dash of unbridled fun. The idea was simple: create a space so vibrant and welcoming that it becomes the preferred choice over other worldly enticements.

"My hope," Pastor Stan expressed one day, "is to weave together moments of joy, friendship, and spiritual sharing. To make our gathering not just a service but a home where all feel seen, loved, and excited to be."

Resourcefulness became our ally in navigating financial hurdles. My dad's fudge, Paul's mom's blueberry cobbler, and Mrs. Matthew's cranberry pineapple upside-down cake became sweet staples at our gatherings and still bring a smile to my face, but we needed real cash for youth activities like retreats and outings. We had to really be resourceful to find money.

During one brainstorming session, Paul pondered, "What if we wash cars for free but get people to pledge donations for each one we do?"

Then we came up with "24-hour-rock-a-thons." At first we didn't know if this would fly, but it was worth trying. The idea was that people would donate for every hour we rocked on rocking chairs without stopping. If one person got a bit dizzy from rocking so much and so long, friends were ready to replace him. We took turns washing cars and rocking in the rocking chair. It was fun because we all did it as a group.

We cheered, rallied, and soon enough, our quirky fundraising ideas, like the aforementioned car washes and amusing rock-a-thons, not only brought in funds but also crafted memories that were cherished and retold in our group.

The result was an enriched journey where we, as a collective, delved into retreats, outings like The Shakespearean Festival in Ashland, Oregon. In addition, we blossomed not just in numbers but in our walks with God.

As teens discovering our paths, we were profoundly impacted by Pastor Stan's genuine investment in our lives, shaping a chapter of safe, exploratory, and spiritually nourishing growth.

9.4 Gravestone

A plan in the heart of a man is like deep water,
But a man of understanding draws it out.
Proverbs 20:5

Another influential person at my church was Jeanine "Mom" Matthews, my junior high Sunday School teacher. She taught at a public school, so she had much experience with kids' issues. She really had a heart for the Job Corps men who came to our church. Those men called her "Mom" Matthews, since she was their mom far away from home. Because of that, we teens also called her "Mom Matthews".

Mom Matthews recognized that in adolescent years, teens had a tendency to become more aware about themselves and about other people's thoughts and feelings toward them. This self-awareness opens up new vulnerabilities and insecurities which can cause selfishness, low self-esteem, depression and poor decision-making.

Secular counselors would have different solutions which would help to some degree; however, Mom Matthews thought the best way to combat adolescent identity crises was to point them toward their purpose in Jesus. When our eyes were fixed on Jesus, we wouldn't be so self-centered, nor would we want people's approval to be our standards of happiness. Instead, we looked to Him for approval by walking in His purpose for His glory.

One Sunday she challenged all of us around the table with this question: "What do you want to be written on your gravestone?"

I thought for a bit and wrote down:

"I want this to be written on my gravestone: 'Here lies a man who made a difference in the world.'"

That one declaration came back into my life when I started college and it has marked the rest of my adult life. God used that innocent declaration to help me live my life with eternity in mind. I desired to make a positive mark in all that I did - big and small.

That was one, most-meaningful, impactful lesson Mom Matthews taught me.

CHAPTER

10

In Search of Identity

For you are all sons of God through faith in Christ Jesus.
Galatians 3:26

10.1 My Sporty and Tough Identity

For we are His workmanship, created in Christ Jesus for good works, which God prepared beforehand so that we would walk in them.
Ephesians 2:10

I knew the Lord had good plans for me, plans for my welfare and not for calamity, plans for a future and a hope. And I knew God created me for His good purpose. I knew He was always watching over me, and protecting me since I was a baby, as a foster child, an orphan, and later as I was adopted into the Pearman family, and also adopted as a child of God.

Yet I had questions about who I was and why He let me exist. Deep inside, just like any other teens out there, I was just barely at the beginning of the process of discovering myself. Although Mom Matthews talked a lot about deep stuff like destiny and purpose in God, I spent a lot of time thinking about how people perceived me and how I would like to be known.

Subconsciously, I wanted to establish my "identity." Deep down, I wanted people to see me as a godly and respectful teen, who was also friendly and outgoing, responsible and hardworking, smart and witty, sporty and tough. In other words, I wanted my winning formula to show and defend who I was. I still didn't know how to let Jesus and His power work in me.

The fall of 1976 was an even bigger adjustment in my life. Not only was I entering my junior high phase of life, but changes happened all around. Even my favorite basketball team, The Portland Trailblazers, were headed to be the NBA champions in the next spring, a first time in Portland's history.

At that time, a "sporty" season also came upon me. The good Lord knew I always wanted to participate in sports, and even though I didn't seek it, He always provided an opportunity to do so. That season was also a testing time for my character.

First, it was just a sporty and fun competition. In Mr. Libby's math class, he mounted a nerf-size, basketball rim. We started to compete with a foam basketball. When the foam basketball got lost or torn, we used wads of paper. We later refined them with masking tape wrappings to make them more spherical, stable basketballs to shoot through the rim. We all took on our favorite Blazers' star names. I was Maurice Lucas, the lean and tough enforcer. My friends were Bill Walton, Lionel Hollins, Bobby Gross, and Dave Twardzick. That made up the starting line-up for the Trail Blazers. Even our math teacher was given a name. We called him Leaping Libby. No doubt about it, Leaping Libby's math class was our favorite class.

Then we did something more competitive. In the seventh grade I started several fun, sport trends. I brought a small rubber ball from home. My friends and I would throw the small, hand-held rubber ball into a very narrow exit-tunnel of the locker room. After one slammed the ball against the wall, the second person would need to catch, then throw it back against the wall as quickly as possible. If a competitor could not catch the ball, then the next person in line would get a turn.

We played this over and over until the recess period ended. Soon others would join in on the fun. If we were not playing this, we would be at the small court outside of the library. I brought my plastic, palm-sized football. We would have five or six friends across from each other on the court. I would start heaving the miniature plastic football as high as I could into the opposing side and see if one of them could catch it, or if not, retrieve it. The one who could retrieve it had a turn to throw it into the air for others to catch. If you could catch it, then you would get 100 points. If you caught it on one bounce, then you would receive 50 points. Whoever accumulated 1,000 points was crowned the champion for that recess period.

There were times where the call to be tough was summoned from within me. One time, one of the upper-class boys who was on the sidelines with his friends retrieved an errant throw. He would not give it back. Even though we asked him to give it back to us, he would not. Nobody would confront him, so for some reason I took it upon myself to confront the bigger upperclassmen. Besides, it was my football.

I ran up to him, looking up at his nose and demanded, "Please return my football!"

"Oh yeah? What would you do about it?" He joked about it and laughed with his friends.

Right then, I just grabbed it right out of his hands and went back to playing. I guess one could say I was not intimidated by bigger boys. In fact, I didn't back down in a fight if I knew I was right. I would not back down on a physical challenge against a bigger person, since I was a fighter.

Another time was when we were playing "Uncle" at school. It was our kind of "strength challenge game." We would clasp one another's hands palm-to-palm and lock our fingers. Then we would bend the friend's fingers backwards and try to get the other person to cry out "uncle" when the pain was unbearable. My opponents were whoever dared to challenge me. One time, I challenged a friend in the seventh grade who was the biggest guy in class at 6'1, 200 lbs. His huge hands tried to lock mine, but I bent his fingers backwards with all my might and persevered in my position until finally my ginormous friend cried "uncle!"

I never lost at that game.

Little did I know that the winning formula that helped me survive in the past started to come up to the surface again. When confronted, I had to be this tough guy. That old identity came up without me knowing.

10.2 My Smart and Responsible Identity

For we are His workmanship, created in Christ Jesus for good works, which God prepared beforehand so that we would walk in them.
Ephesians 2:10

I always prided myself as being a smart and responsible person. I might not make it to the athletic teams because of my physical challenges from polio, but I was smart and responsible, which was my other winning formula to survive and thrive.

The following year, I liked this girl who was already on the student council. So, I got up enough courage to try to run for the student officer position. I had to make a speech to state why I should be an eighth-grade officer for the entire second lunch period assembly at the cafeteria. I spoke, but I was not chosen. Surprisingly, a girl from my elementary school made it into the position. Somehow, I never thought she would be popular enough.

That experience hurt my identity. I was depending on my own strength and not on the Lord, but I couldn't see it. I wasn't pursuing the student council position to make a difference but to impress the girl and be popular. I probably didn't prepare my best anyway, but the sting of that rejection, like Pandora's Box, opened up a lot of insecurities in me. My view about myself, that I was a likable person - because I was smart, responsible, kind, tough, and decent - was shaken. After that experience, I became more introspective and less outgoing throughout my teen years. I still liked the other girl, but I never did anything about it for the rest of my life. I feared being rejected by her. I only looked from a distance.

It was painful to realize that my winning formula failed me again. I couldn't depend on it like I thought. Despite this, I still didn't connect to Jesus, who overcomes all troubles and temptations, and yet without sin.

10.3 Be Still, My Soul

He says, "Be still, and know that I am God;
I will be exalted among the nations,
I will be exalted on the earth."
Psalm 46: 10 ESV

When I was not trying to be "somebody," the Lord paved a way to elevate me. When I was not chosen, He chose me. His thoughts were higher than my thoughts, and His ways higher than mine, but I didn't realize this truth until much later on.

Eighth grade was the year I joined the eighth-grade boys' red basketball team; not as a player, but as the manager. This was how the Lord landed it into my lap.

Mr. Wakefield was the 8th grade boys' basketball coach and my career study teacher. I really enjoyed his class, because he liked to talk about interesting things like what jobs would be like in the future with the technological boom that was going to transform the American workplace. He also discussed new things I had never heard of - like computers that were being made to replace typewriters. I hadn't even mastered using the typewriter yet let alone the computer. His class really stimulated my curiosity and imagination of technology.

I was especially interested in the career skills assessment. I heard about one part of the assessment where we would fill out this hand-eye assessment as fast as we could. When I got into his class to take the test, my competitive spirit was awakened, so I was pumped up to break the record. I raced through the sheet as fast as I could, and I set the new record. After that Mr. Wakefield retold my story to all his classes with so much exaggeration that made me sheepishly embarrassed. Then he called me to stay after class.

"David, sorry if I embarrassed you a little today, but I was genuinely impressed. I was thinking maybe you could help me be the manager for our basketball team. I chose you because this job would suit you well, since you are a meticulous person when it comes to details and responsibility. What do you think about that?"

I was so excited, but I said, "Let me ask my parents about it and let you know tomorrow. Thank you for the opportunity."

Maybe he chose me because I passed that hand-eye assessment, but my parents agreed it was the favor of the Lord. They believed the fact that I had been faithful and responsible was why Mr. Wakefield offered me the position. I was so touched to see the way the Lord rewarded me when I didn't even expect that to happen, especially after trying to make things "happen" on my own strength.

So, I accepted the challenge as a manager. The Lord knew I loved basketball and how much sports meant to me, especially since I was not able to run with my leg. It was as if He wanted to tell me He hadn't forgotten me. I was amazed that again and again, my Gracious Lord in His infinite wisdom provided a way for me to be part of the basketball team.

Of course, this prestigious position came with plenty of hard labor and sacrifices. The practice was at 7am, and that meant I had to get up by 6am to get ready and walk 30 minutes to arrive before it started. I was in charge of sweeping the floor which involved pushing a wide gym sweeper wrapped in wet white towels. Fortunately, the sweeper conveniently did a 2-in-1 job of sweeping and mopping at the same time.

Then there were more responsibilities. I was in charge of tending to the racks full of basketballs. I collected all the basketballs, towels, and equipment before and after the practice. I was also in charge of the scorebook for our team during games. I really didn't mind all the responsibilities required because I wanted my position to be meaningful and useful.

My hard work and sacrifice paid off. It was so rewarding to be part of the basketball team. I was even part of the official team picture that would go in the yearbook. On the other hand, a small part of me felt I could shoot better than some of the players who made the team. I had to silence that thought with the best method: gratefulness.

Since I accomplished my job as a manager so well, Mr. Wakefield recommended me to the 9th grade coach to be the lead manager for the 9th grade team which combined both the red and white team into one roster. The only thing different that year was that an assistant manager was chosen to help me out.

The Lord was true when He said, "Be still and know that I am the Lord." Not only did He land me a good position and experience being a manager, but also, He rewarded my faithfulness beyond what I could ask or imagine. This year was the first time in my life I would own my own genuine Nike™

leather basketball shoes. My family could never afford a pair, but a donor had given the entire 9th grade team Nike leather high top basketball shoes.

It was a moment I would cherish as a youth. Yes, it was a period of joy and pride. More important in my life story, it was another way for God to let me know that His eye was on me, His precious child, His sparrow. When I trusted Him, He. made a way that was way better than my own. I just needed to be still and let God be God.

10.4 When My Winning Formula Fails

But now, O Lord, You are our Father,
We are the clay, and You are our potter;
And all of us are the work of Your hand.
Isaiah 64:8

The Lord gave me so much favor in the eighth grade that I was also chosen to be in the annual class. We were in charge of putting together the yearbook for junior high. This job entailed taking pictures of events, making the layouts for the yearbook, and creating page designs from cover to cover. There was a guideline for each of those important tasks.

I was assigned to cover the eighth-grade football team. I clicked many pictures at the last football game of the season with the school's manual SLR camera.

Mr. Libby, our class advisor, had warned us about the SLR camera. It was the most popular camera of the '70s. It had interchangeable lenses in the front and a viewfinder in back to look through the lens to check the picture with some help from a mirror inside.

"Hey kids, listen carefully: if for some reason after the roll is done and while the roll is being rewound, the film breaks in the middle of the rewind, don't open the camera's back," Mr. Libby warned us.

To my horror, the very thing that he told us to avoid happened on my watch. When I almost finished rewinding the roll, the camera suddenly made that plasticky, tearing sound. I thought, *did the film break?*, but I kept rewinding a bit more until there was no more resistance to show the film roll had rewound. Since I still needed to take some more pictures, I opened the back of the camera to change the film. To my shock, I saw the film was torn in half and the negatives were exposed.

My heart dropped. *Oh God, please help me*, I prayed as I ran to take it back to our dark room. But it was too late. I discovered all the negatives had been exposed to the light, and all my pictures were ruined.

143

The next day, I confessed my blunder to Mr. Libby. Of course, he was not happy, but he tried to console me, since I was quite disturbed by the mishap. We had a challenge on our hands, since that was the last football game for the eighth-grade white football team. I couldn't afford to waste time crying over spilled milk. I switched modes to solution-finding. My head was thinking, and at the same time my heart was praying hard. That very minute God gave me the idea. I proposed to Mr. Libby an "end-around football play" to work around the challenge. I suggested we look for pictures from the seventh-grade football season and insert them as eighth grade.

"Well, David, good job for thinking of that brilliant solution," Mr. Libby nodded approvingly, since we didn't have any other solution. I was able to find enough pictures of the players to fill the page. The rest of the yearbook went without a hitch for all of us.

When it was over, I breathed a quick prayer of thankfulness to God for helping me solve my blunder. He truly caused all things to work together for good, even my blunder.

Slowly I learned that if I let Him be the potter, and I surrendered myself as His clay, then He would work all things well into my life. Whether it was something good He had started in me or even a blunder I made, He would create something beautiful out of the mix. I was working so hard, trying to search and establish my identity with my own strength, trying to be who I wanted to be, whom I wanted to be known for, and I failed.

What I needed to do was just to be still and submit to the Potter. Then He could mold me into His beautiful vessel, still imperfect, but perfect in His eyes through Jesus.

10.5 Jesus as My New Identity, My True Winner

I have been crucified with Christ; and it is no longer I who live, but Christ lives in me; and the life which I now live in the flesh I live by faith in the Son of God, who loved me and gave Himself up for me.
Galatians 2: 20

In search of my identity, I was inadvertently trying to mold myself based on my winning formula. First, I wanted to be sporty and tough, and the Lord did graciously give me a sporty season to enjoy. But behind this winning formula there was a dark side. Whenever I was confronted, I turned and became an ugly tough monster who refused to be defeated. I had a hard time feeling compassion for others, because I had to defend myself all the time by being tough. I was not given mercy, so I didn't need to give out mercy.

Then I hid behind being smart and responsible to compensate for my polio that caused me not to be athletic. This winning formula also failed me, since it didn't help me to be likable and popular as I wanted to be, with people in general and especially with girls. It also didn't help me avoid blunders even though I tried hard to be perfect in all my responsibilities.

I tried to win with my own strengths, with my own made-up winning formula, and I still lost. And when I didn't try to win with my own strength, the Lord showed up. He gently elevated me and gave me favors when I was undeserving. When I made blunders too, He was the Potter who reworked me—the clay, with all the good and bad parts that happened in me—into something beautiful.

With Jesus, I didn't need a winning formula. He won the victory already. His winning formula was just love—love for me and all humans. Love took Him to the cross. With His love, He defeated death, the devil, and sin, and made a comeback through His resurrection. Jesus didn't need a winning formula. He was, is, and will be the Winner, always and forever. Now He invited me to be on His winning team. The imperfect disciples joined His

145

team a long time ago and like a Potter, He molded each one to be more like Him day by day.

I was tired of running my life by myself. Yes, I accepted Jesus in 6th grade, but after that I was still running my old life with my own broken winning formula as the fuel. My formula was good, and God gave these strengths to me, but I wasn't supposed to rely on them and make them my identity. Step-by step, the Lord revealed to me what I needed to do with them. He wanted me to completely surrender all these strengths to Him and let Him take over my life utterly and in all aspects: my identity, dreams and aspirations. After all, I was a child of the almighty, all-loving God and adopted into His family. He would be my identity and my winning formula that could not fail me.

However, to switch from my old habits of relying on the old winning formula to new habits of depending on Jesus as my new Identity would be a process in the years to come, as Jesus the Potter patiently molded me as a clay in His hand. As I waited for the process, I basked in the truth that "Jesus is the Winner, and I'm on the Winning Side!"

CHAPTER

11

The Ups and Downs of

High School Life

Be of sober spirit, be on the alert. Your adversary, the devil,
prowls around like a roaring lion, seeking someone to devour.
But resist him, firm in your faith, knowing that the same
experiences of suffering are being accomplished by your brethren
who are in the world.
1 Peter 5:8-9

11.1 The Late '70s and Early '80s Era

Set your mind on the things above, not on the things that are on earth.
Colossians 3:2

Now that I was in high school, I started to pay attention to life outside of myself, my family, church, and school. My eyes were opened to the cultures, news from America and around the world, popular trends, movies, songs, and even a bit of politics. Basically, I was trying to keep up with what society in general was doing. I was still interested in school, youth activities at church, and sports, but suddenly my attention was divided because I didn't want to be left out from what my friends were talking about.

The end of the '70s to early '80s was a fun era. It was marked by pop culture where everything seemed happy, light, and entertaining. I didn't care for the hippie part. Many girls started wearing bell-bottom pants and super high heels because they were popular.

Star Wars™ came out in 1977 and was a huge success. Disco was a thing because John Travolta made it popular with his film, *Saturday Night Fever*©. Everyone I knew wanted to dance with his disco moves. He became very popular. In 1978, his movie *Grease*© came out where he starred with Olivia Newton John. It was a musical with lots of singing and dancing. Most of my friends watched it, but my very conservative mother didn't allow me to watch it. I was sullen for several days. Songs from the Bee Gees, like *Staying Alive*© and *How Deep is Your Love*© were also popular. My friends and I sang that like we had someone to love already. And there was this anticipation of the future, what the '80s would bring.

11.2 Adjusting to High School

But the Lord is faithful, and He will strengthen and protect you
from the evil one.
2 Thessalonians 3:3

Entering the 10th grade was possibly the most challenging of my teen years. I came in with a range of feelings, from the high of excitement to the low of apprehension about the unknowns. I couldn't decide whether I was excited or anxious.

In some ways, high school life was the same. When we got bored, we carved words or our initials on the wooden desks, even the new ones, without our teachers knowing. We passed notes to friends as a way to communicate in class. We had to borrow books from the library for research. Calculators were coming in, but they were still expensive, and teachers taught on chalkboards, so chalk powder always found its way to our hands or pants.

In other ways, you could feel the peer pressure way more intensely than in the junior high years. We focused on getting girls' attention by being either in sports or in leadership. Of course, I had to keep up with being a smart guy. The guys were still wearing incredibly short shorts for gym time. I stayed with rope climbing and sweatpants. Girls idolized Farah Fawcett from *Charlie's Angels*©, so they got their hair to look just like hers and spent forever in the bathroom to fix it.

I did well in academics, and I had friends at church and school, but no one to call my buddy to do things outside of school time. I began to feel lonely and unwanted.

Despite the trepidation of a new school, I did experience some fascinating moments during the tenth grade. One of which was in a math lecture with Mr. Crossfield and over 110 students.

As Mr. Crossfield started explaining how to derive the quadratic formula, he started to loosen up his necktie. I thought maybe the tie had felt uncomfortable around his neck. He laid the tie on the side of the lecture table. Then he proceeded to unbutton his collared shirt.

I looked at my friend Joe and he gave me a puzzled look. I was thinking, *wait a minute; what kind of class is this?* All of this unveiling was happening while he lectured on each step of the derivation.

Mr. Crossfield was not done. He removed his shirt and laid it aside. There before us, in front of 110 captivated students, was Mr. Crossfield with all the steps of deriving the quadratic equation on his front and back, not on his bare chest but on a white t-shirt.

I did enjoy that math class. The class was split up into lectures and four homeroom classes. The lecture was formally seated to honor those who were the top ten in the class after each term. I relished the opportunity for a friendly competition. We had four terms, so we were assigned seating on the next three terms based on rank. I never did get to sit in seat number one, but I did get to see the back of the person who was in seat number one.

The second unforgettable moment of tenth grade also came from Mr. Crossfield.

Mr. Crossfield was also my home room teacher. Since I loved math, I kept a nice table of my scores so I could see how I was doing in the class. I never purposely showed it to anyone, but Mr. Crossfield must have seen it.

At one point after class, Mr. Crossfield talked to me about my score keeping. He said he loved how organized I was in keeping my scores, and he wondered if I would keep scores for his tenth-grade boys' basketball team. That meant I would go on the road with the team as we traveled on the school bus to rival teams in other towns nearby. I liked basketball, and I liked it even more since I got to participate in my own way. God again showed how He could arrange everything just at His fingertips to bless the desire of my heart. To this day, basketball is my favorite sport.

God used my two favorite things in school, math and basketball, to help me feel at ease to start the first year of my high school life. He was such a good God, and His eyes were truly on me.

11.3 Spiritual Attack!

Submit therefore to God. Resist the devil and he will flee from you.
James 4: 7

One month after I started high school, both of my parents were in the hospital for various reasons at the same time. I needed to stay with my mom's friend. The good thing was my mom's friend lived almost next-door to the high school.

This was not planned, at least for my mom. My dad had a scheduled procedure for his leg to ease the blood flow. On the other hand, my mom could not sleep at all for five straight days. Mom had signed up for a special ministry dealing with suicide prevention. She didn't ask other people to cover and intercede for her in prayer, so she encountered spiritual attacks right after that. She was being harassed by demonic forces after several days of not sleeping. She was able to see demons running around the house and everywhere she looked. She became paranoid of her surroundings as they were so real to her.

Dad and I asked the pastors and elders of our church to pray. We didn't ask the prayer chain since this was a bit of a sensitive issue. At one point, my dad and I cried helplessly. We even confessed any sins we could think of openly to God in front of each other, but she was still under heavy attacks.

On Sunday afternoon, we were planning to go hear David Wilkerson speak at the Douglas County Fairgrounds. We wanted to bring her there to see if somebody from the team could pray for my mom. As we drove, my mom screamed, "No, no, don't turn right, turn left, turn left!" We were startled so we started driving up the hill. Then she directed us to steep Winter Street past the house that belonged to the kids I took care of one summer. She said, "They are after us, keep going, keep going!" We ended up at the little clearing at the top of the hill.

As we parked on the top, she warned, "We can't go back to the house. They are burning it down now." We were confused, trying to figure out what we should do, when a couple walked up the entrance of the hill. Mom yelled,

"They are coming for us," in a frantic, hopeless voice. She became more frantic and louder.

We didn't know what to do. In desperation, I peered directly into her troubled eyes and commanded in a firm voice: "In JESUS' name, get out demons!" Suddenly, Mom's body collapsed into my dad's arms and then she said in a soft, calm voice to me, "You're a prophet."

She was back to being my mom again. We were all quiet, trying to process the whole incident. We had no doubt it was the power of Jesus' name that rebuked the demons and caused them to flee. Plus, we were exhausted mentally, emotionally, physically, and spiritually.

Dad and I drove my mom back to the house. Immediately, Dad called the doctor, who said she needed to be admitted to the hospital since she hadn't slept for that long. We gathered some of her things and took her to Mercy Medical Center, the nearest hospital on the north side. She had to be monitored there for several weeks until she could recuperate. A few days later, my dad had to go in for at least a week or more for his procedure, so Dad made an arrangement for me to stay with their friend. At least my mom and dad were at the same hospital, and I could visit them on the same trip.

That day was the second time in my life that I cried out "JESUS" in desperation! The first time I cried Jesus, He rescued me from the family in Michigan. This time I saw the demonstration of God's power in a different light. Jesus answered our prayers for my mom and delivered my family from the hideous dark powers. I will forever remember that day. Knowing that God could make the demons flee in a real way gave me faith to pray for complete healing for both of my parents.

Jesus, You truly WON the victory over the devil and his power!

11.4 Prayer for a Lonely Heart

The righteous cry, and the LORD hears
And delivers them out of all their troubles.
The LORD is near to the brokenhearted
And saves those who are crushed in spirit.
Psalm 34: 17-18

Tenth grade was the year I ever earnestly prayed for my first best buddy. I was feeling lonelier than ever in my life. My first and last best friend was Seong-ho, way back then when I was in the Holt orphanage. Here in America, I had friends at school and in the youth group at church, but I had no close friends to confide in or to hang out with after school or church. I spent too many lunch breaks in solitude at the library, eating my sandwich and reading my small New Testament, not so no one would bother me, but because I didn't have close friends to hang out with just for the sake of hanging out.

I didn't know that feeling lonely was common to many teenagers. The part of the teen brain that regulates emotions was still maturing in us, so the impact of loneliness became more intense. We were way more emotional, and this was felt by girls and boys as well.

Socially, we longed to belong and be accepted as part of a group identity. When we were alone, we might feel that everyone else was having a great time and we were excluded, unwanted, alienated, or separated. This was so painful. In fact, I knew a friend or two who didn't know how to cope with loneliness and ended up with anxiety and depression.

The good thing that came out of my mom's incident was that I believed in the power of prayer in Jesus' name because I experienced it. I stopped striving with the old winning formula but looked to Jesus as my Source of everything that I needed.

So I prayed, "Lord, You know how lonely I am. Would you bring me a friend that I can be a buddy with, so I can have a best friend? I ask this in Jesus' Name. Amen."

I prayed each night before bedtime and each morning when I went to school. Still no friend. Sometimes the sting of all my rejections came back -

from my childhood as an orphan, to being a foster child, and to the fact that my first adoption didn't work out. The devil played those stories over and over in my mind and told me the lie that no one wanted to be my close friend. *Yes, who would want to spend time with me? I am invisible.* Not invisible as my superpower, but no one really saw me.

My heart started to ache. The devil wanted to put doubts that God wasn't going to give me a best friend. I kept praying. My faith might be only as small as a mustard seed; I did have doubts here and there, but I wasn't going to stop praying.

After about six months into that year, I bumped into an acquaintance named Brian Fuller at a Christian club called Campus Life. I didn't attend the club that often my first year. The club met at 7:17pm on Tuesdays at a host's home or at the school. The meeting was set at a weird time so we would remember and be on time. It was so good to know that he was also a Christian. Most of my friends weren't Christians, since we went to a public school.

I became good friends with Brian Fuller. We found out we were in the big lecture class for algebra and English together. He was truly God's answer to prayer for me. We became fast friends all the way through high school graduation. Our friendship was organic and a mutual blessing to each other.

Once Brian got his driver's license, he picked me up many times. We were able to hang out at Campus Life, at games, in each other's homes, or at some Christian activity. We were truly best friends. We each went to our separate colleges after Roseburg High, but we tried to correspond for the first year. Even though we really haven't kept in touch since high school, I will always treasure our friendship during those years. God really answered my prayers for a best friend.

11.5 The Downward Spiral of Discontentment

He brought me up out of the pit of destruction, out of the miry clay,
And He set my feet upon a rock making my footsteps firm.
Psalm 40:2

High school also brought out my dark side. I began longing to have what my other teen friends had. My parents provided for what I needed, and I was truly blessed by living in a loving family, but why was my heart so dissatisfied?

I started comparing my life with my friends' lives, and without realizing it, I fell into the trap of discontentment. I became bitter, envious, and jealous of their lives. Why did they have it so easy? Even Brian Fuller could use his parents' cars. My mom didn't allow me to drive her car, even though I had already taken the driver's ed course. Now, I wasn't asking for a car. I thought I was already a considerate son to my parents. I would not ask for crazy and expensive items. All my friends were able to follow the trends and wear nice clothes. I dreamed of wearing some brand name clothes or at least the clothes that were in fashion for teens. I imagined I would be more accepted if I wore those nice, dark corduroy pants, and alternated them with white baggy, pleated pants that movie stars wore as they strolled on the beaches. And of course, I needed the Levi's™ jeans. I was not able to get even one pair, nor any of those things. I tried to reason with my mom many times. It never worked. I grew more frustrated. Instead, my mom bought me what I called "Monkey Ward's" department store specials. I was exasperated.

"Mom, do you really love me? Do you even care about what I feel? I really get embarrassed wearing these pants. Why can't you buy me those Levi's™ I told you about? They're on sale. You know I'll take good care of them." I tried to lower my voice so no one would hear our embarrassing conversation.

But she just said matter-of-factly, "No, David, I told you those are too expensive." I didn't hear any compassion or empathy like I thought any Christian mom should have.

I became so resentful. On the car ride home, my math brain tried to calculate how much my mom could have saved from giving all those dollars to random waiters, to the church, to the suicide-prevention organization, to the Holt adoption agency so they could afford to care for more children in the orphanage, to many Christian organizations, and to countless homeless people on the street. I knew she supported so many organizations because every month she'd get letters with envelopes from them to give again the following month. That was the cycle of her generosity. She could afford to buy me decent clothes if she wanted to, but instead, she had to support all those. I started feeling unloved, unprioritized, and unheard.

At home, I would get into heated squabbles with my mom. "You do all those good things, but you don't care about my needs. Why did you even adopt me?"

I also tried the soft way, saying, "Mom, if you just looked at my solution then you would see that it would be doable and not too much of a burden." But Mom wouldn't budge.

I looked at Dad, and his face showed he didn't want to be in between the two of us.

When nothing worked, I was filled with anger and self-pity. From my mouth came manipulative and terrible words: "If you don't love me anymore, just give me a knife. I don't want to live anymore. I want to kill myself!"

These scenarios usually happened during my earlier to mid-teen years. I must have been a pain in that time period. My parents loved me unconditionally and had always provided everything I needed, but it was so easy for me to take everything for granted. I was focusing on myself so much.

Thank God I grew out of those teen years. My parents must have prayed a lot. Slowly my heart became tender again. God truly lifted me out of the pit of despair, out of the mud of worldly wants, and the miry clay of covetousness and discontentment. Then He set my feet on solid ground and steadied me as I walked along.

In those tender moments, the Lord showed me that I hadn't been keeping my relationship with Him. He wanted to be my best friend all along; I only treated Him as an on-call person. I would call on Him when I needed something desperately, like the time when I wanted to have a friend. I didn't seek Him diligently like I should have. Right then, I decided I didn't want to have a spiritual life that could easily go up and down like a yo-yo. So, I prayed to God to help me be steady, and to walk on solid ground.

CHAPTER

12

Grow Me Deeper,

Take Me Higher

Abide in Me, and I in you. As the branch cannot bear fruit of itself unless it abides in the vine, so neither can you unless you abide in Me. I am the vine, you are the branches; he who abides in Me and I in him, he bears much fruit, for apart from Me you can do nothing.
John 15: 4-5

12.1 The Fourth Dimension of Faith

If you abide in Me, and My words abide in you, ask whatever you wish, and it will be done for you.
John 15: 7

As a child, I had memorized verses in John 15, but now my heart was hungry to know Him deeper. I was glad I had to go through those dark teen issues so I could see how I needed God to desperately cut the junk out of my life. All my life, I had been using my winning formula, to be smart, strong, and independent in order to survive and thrive. It wasn't until recently that I began to learn to depend on Him completely to win in this life.

"Jesus, You are the vine and the Master Gardener. I want to abide in You, Lord. I give You permission to prune all the sinful things inside of me so I can bear much fruit for you. Take all the unfruitful branches so they won't grow inside of me," I prayed sincerely.

God was preparing me to grow deeply rooted in Him so He could take me higher in my faith journey.

Not long after that, my mom introduced me to *The Fourth Dimension©* by Paul Yonggi Cho (1979, Logos International) while I was eating cereal in the kitchen.

"Son, you might like this book by Pastor Paul Yonggi Cho. He is a great minister from South Korea who has so much faith in growing his congregation. Now he has 500,000 members," Mom said, trying to promote the book to me since I wasn't so fond of reading.

"500,000 members? Wow. I can't imagine," I said, since our church in Roseburg only had around 200 members.

"Yes, I know. Isn't that so amazing? God gave him a vision for a large church and the strategy to grow their members. The key is the members flourish and grow because they are deeply planted in cell groups, small group Bible studies," Mom explained.

"The title is more interesting to me, Mom. To have the fourth dimension is very intriguing to me." I was keener about the title, not the author.

"Why is it, son? I know you love math, but I don't understand what the big deal is." Mom now was interested in my explanation.

I got my Rubik's™ cube out from my drawer in my room and went back to the kitchen.

"See this cube, Mom? A cube in the zero dimension would be only this point. It represents a point in space, but it has no dimension at all. It has no length, no depth, and no height." I pointed at a corner of the cube. My mom nodded.

"Now, if we add length to this point, then it becomes a line. In the first dimension, everything exists as a line. So, a cube in the first dimension would look like a line, but with no width value nor height value. So, in math, when I move it horizontally like this, I am making a line in the x direction." I moved my finger horizontally from the first point to the other point in the corner to show my mom I was making a line. My mom nodded again.

"Now in the second dimension, we can add the width value perpendicularly to the length. In math we said we moved in x and y directions. Our cube would look like a square in the second dimension." I pointed to one side of the cube to show it was a flat square to demonstrate the second dimension. My mom smiled.

"Now in order to have a cube we need to have the height as well. In math when we add the third dimension, the square now gets extruded in a third perpendicular direction or the z direction. So now the cube can properly be called the cube because it has the dimensions of length, width, and height," I explained as simply as I could.

My mom looked so proud of me.

"I know a cube in the fourth dimension is called a tesseract [a four-dimensional hypercube, or "4 cube"], but I don't know anything about it. I am also very curious how knowing this math concept has helped Pastor Cho with growing his church." Explaining to mom made me super excited to read.

Pastor Cho shared in his book that basically the fourth dimension is about faith. Faith entails a powerful prayer life. Prayer life needs powerful faith. Both must work together in our lives in order to see the fruit of our prayers. Faith happens when we depend on the power of the Holy Spirit, and not our own strength.

He also had a chapter about the creative power of the spoken word. Many times, we would cancel what we asked in prayer because our faithless words negated our prayer. He made me aware to watch what I said, and to ask the Holy Spirit to pray with confidence and faith in Him. This kind of faith would help us overcome all spiritual battles and hindrances in our lives, so we would grow and bear much fruit, for His glory and purpose.

It was like abiding in the vine that Jesus spoke about to me earlier through John 15. My soul was refreshed, and my faith was renewed. I was inspired to develop that kind of dynamic faith and to be bold in asking Him, as long as my motive was right. I wanted my faith to be in the fourth dimension. Not the math's fourth dimension, but faith's kind. So, I decided to ask God in faith.

To put it into practice, I was inspired to dream for a new, beautiful, blue, 10-speed Schwinn™ racer. Pastor Cho said I had to be very specific, so I was very specific with my dream bike. I didn't tell anyone about it. I just prayed in my heart and tried to abide in Him. I confessed my desire and believed the Lord would give it to me if He saw it in His will.

The following week my dad said suddenly that they had been praying, and they wanted to buy me a Schwinn™ bicycle.

I couldn't believe it. The Lord answered my prayer!

We went straight down to the Schwinn™ store, and I saw the bike I imagined. Without hesitation, my parents paid for the bike for me.

That blue bike served me faithfully through my high school years, my part time jobs, and all the way to college years. That bike survived through two run-ins with cars. Both of those times God protected me from serious injuries.

Getting my bike was a powerful experience that helped me see that God actually took pleasure in blessing His children. Just like parents who get more excited to see their children being happy when opening their Christmas gifts, God is delighted when His children enjoy His blessings. He is delighted because He loves us, and not because of our own merits. It is His grace all the way.

12.2 He Watches Over Me

So do not fear; you are more valuable than many sparrows.
Matthew 10:31

Ever since I prayed to God to help me abide in Him, and for my faith to be strong and not up and down like a yo-yo, I became more and more aware of His presence in my life. I could feel God was always watching over me. And He always was, even during an accident.

I was a junior in high school, working at a gas station in my town during the summer. There were three part-time employees including myself. The crazy thing was we were all named Dave. There was Jumbo Dave, Dave, and Mini Dave. You could guess who the Mini Dave was. My shift was from late afternoon to 10pm that week.

It was my turn to close the gas station, so I was there the last few hours by myself. In our little town there weren't many people stopping for gas in the late hours, so it made sense to only have one person working. I was trying to close the shop quickly because it was already past 10pm. Then I could hop on my blue racer for the uphill trek to my home two miles away.

As I was pushing one of the tire tracks from gas pump island one, I was not careful to watch my left fingers as I approached the left side of the garage doorway. The tire rack hit a dip and my fingers got sandwiched between the side of the steel rack and the steel door jam. I screamed in pain and knelt to the floor.

Blood started to pour out of my hand. Since I took first-aid, I knew I needed to stop the bleeding. I found a clean rag and started to wrap it as tightly as I could with my right hand and my mouth. I tried to keep my hand above my heart.

But I still needed to finish the closing. "Lord, help!" I said. Somehow, I didn't have any fear; knowing He watches over me gave me so much peace that I would be alright.

Right at that moment, I saw a small sedan pull up to the far island. I actually had already turned off the lights to the islands and turned off the pumps to show we were closed. As I hobbled over to the car, a middle-aged lady got out. Ignoring my pain, I breathed out to her that the station was closed.

She noticed my bandaged left hand full of blood. I explained my accident. The lady then replied, "I can take you to the emergency room." I was surprised by her generosity to a stranger. Of course, I took her compassionate offer.

But I still needed to close the gas station properly. Holding my pain like a brave soldier, I finished securing the building before locking the door. I called home to tell my dad of my accident. My sweet dad kindly said he would pick me up, but I stopped him by saying God sent me an angel under the guise of a kind woman.

God was watching over me by sending this lady. He knew I was going to have an accident, so He sent help ahead of time and arranged for her to arrive at the gas station at just the right time. After that I never heard from that lady again. Maybe she really was an angel.

12.3 Healing for My Disappointments

He heals the brokenhearted
And binds up their wounds.
Psalm 147: 3

I found God was not only so good at binding the physical wounds, but at also binding the emotional ones.

Some of my friends had started dating. I was shyer at talking to girls, let alone asking them for a date. But just like any other teens, I was intrigued by the prospect of a romantic relationship, even if I had to keep it to myself.

I made some of my own money and saved up. With my savings, I bought my first stereo system. Even my well-to-do brother-in-law replied, "I never had a stereo as nice as this one." Maybe he was excited for me. I felt so proud of that moment because I had earned it with my own sweat.

After school and between jobs I'd turn on the stereo, put on some music, and sing along. When doing house tasks like washing dishes and vacuuming, I'd pretend I was singing to a girl. I sang in the bathroom so long that my mom had to knock to remind me not to waste so much water. I memorized so many love songs. Some of my favorites were *Annie's Song*© and *Leavin' on a Jet Plane*© , by John Denver; *Both Sides Now*© , by Judy Collins; *Dancing Queen*© , by ABBA; *Feelings*© , by Morris Albert; *Goodbye Girl*© , by David Gates; *Honesty*© , by Billy Joel; *Hotel California*© , by the Eagles; *How Deep is Your Love*© , by the Bee Gees; *I'll Be There*© , by the Jackson 5; *I will Survive*© , by Gloria Gaynor; *Nobody Does It Better*© , by Carly Simon, and *Yesterday Once More*© , by The Carpenters.

I was a hopeless romantic with the songs I liked. But I had no girl yet to love and be loved.

Soon Pastor Stan got married and left. Another couple stepped up to be our youth leaders. After one youth service in the evening, the wife teased me and my friend saying, "She would have gone on a date *even with you guys*, if you guys asked me." Maybe she was trying to encourage us to find dates, but we were quite offended. How could she say "even with you guys," as if we were lower than everyone else?

The girl she was talking about was a homecoming queen in my high school who was in our youth group. She was beautiful and godly, and yes, she probably would go out with me or my friend if we would just ask, but it was not nice for the youth leader to use the word "even."

Yes, I was excited about the possibility of asking for a date with the prettiest girl. Just knowing her from our youth activities together, I knew she would probably be kind and gracious to have a little date with me. I was still too insecure to ask.

I thought about my leg. Who would want to go out with someone who had physical effects from polio? I thought about my height, and all of the sudden I had a flash of the faces of all those handsome and athletic tall guys who were in my school. I thought about being Asian. There were only a few Asians in my high school, but I purposely avoided them. I didn't want to be associated with them because I had a past in Korea as an orphan where people rejected me. Why would anyone want to be with me, a person with an unknown past?

My mom often said I had a handsome face, a smart brain, and most importantly, a beautiful heart. Yes, all moms would say that about their sons, wouldn't they? Her compliment didn't console me that much. I was always clean and neat since being in the orphanage, and by high school I had grown muscles in my arms. I'd like to think I was manly. I was helpful, smart, resourceful, kind, gentle, and naturally very caring and sensitive to others, but for some reason my physical attributes and personality traits were never good enough in my mind to be confident in front of girls.

That was my dating life or non-dating life, to be exact.

That summer, I did fall in love with another beautiful, sweet girl named Cindy from my high school youth group. Her parents were active members of the church, so they would host our youth group sometimes. They lived in a beautiful yellow house in the countryside. There was a swing on the front porch and Cindy and I would sit together swinging and talking. It was always so easy to talk to one another.

When the summer was over, my heart was broken because she told me she was going to move away to Montana with her family. She was really the best. I wasn't looking for a girlfriend, but we just connected so well when we conversed. She liked my wit, and I enjoyed her stories. Why did this have to stop?

I dreamed of singing *Nobody Does It Better*© to her before she left, but I got so nervous because of the word "baby" in that song. I wrote the lyrics in my first letter, hoping she knew what I meant. Every time the lyrics said "baby" I changed it to "Cindy".

We tried to communicate regularly through letters, but it was a challenge. She started to open up to me by sharing her struggles, and I tried to encourage her, but after a while, it was hard to keep the long-distance relationship alive. Then the letters stopped coming from her.

I didn't know what happened. Did she stop liking me? Did she like someone else? Did her parents tell her to stop writing to me? Had she been writing to me because she only had a pity on me, and did not actually like me? Was she or was she not authentic with her feelings for me?

I was heartbroken. I was puzzled. I tried to forget the relationship and focus on my school, church, and job. The song, *Honesty*© from Billy Joel really described my disappointment and heartbreak: "Honesty is such a lonely word…"

Then, out of the blue, a year later, she sent me a letter from Eugene, Oregon. Eugene and Roseburg were less than a one hour's drive. I was ecstatic. I started to write to her again. She replied that she and her family were coming down to Roseburg and would be in church one Sunday. I couldn't believe my eyes.

That Sunday, I wore my best clothes, a buttoned blue denim shirt, and made sure I was neat and ready. I was in a combination of feeling proud, nervous, and red-cheeked to sit with her. It had been such a long time since I had been able to sit together with her. I wished that the clock would stop and we could spend more time together. We promised to keep writing to each other, but again, after a few months, the letters were far between, and the relationship ended the following year.

This time I was not as broken-hearted since God comforted me to make it through. Either that, or I protected the walls of my heart from another disappointment by not hoping. When you were not hoping, you couldn't be disappointed. I remembered that God was close to me when I was broken-hearted the first time.

That reminded me of my own salvation story when I said "yes" to Him. God waited so long for me to be ready for Him. So patiently. God, Himself, also doesn't force anyone to love Him. God doesn't force anyone to repent. God offers the invitation and waits. He waits like the father of the prodigal son. God waits like a just king who expects obedience from his subjects. He waits like the bridegroom for His bride to be ready.

I wanted Cindy to say "yes" to me. I was hoping she would be mine forever.

"Yes" is the word that God longs to hear from the sinners, and He is relentless at pursuing each of them, me included. And God wanted me to be His forever.

For the first time, I understood this heartache like I understood a bit of the heart of God.

"Jesus, no matter whether I would have a girl or not in the future, You will always be my first love in my heart. No one can take this place of Yours in my heart," I wrote in my journal.

12.4 Healing for My Brokenness

Therefore I am well content with weaknesses, with insults, with distresses, with persecutions, with difficulties, for Christ's sake; for when I am weak, then I am strong.
2 Corinthians 12: 10

In my junior year in high school, I was accepted into the prestigious *a Capella* choir class. This was different from our choir at church, so it was quite an opportunity for me. Our choir teacher, Mr. Hodson, would sit on a bench at the piano and get us to warm up our vocal cords: by singing, "Mississippi, Mississippi… Mississippi mud!" one note, higher and higher key, over and over. Then we would start our practice.

Joining a choir was more than just learning to sing with other people. Our coach couldn't emphasize enough the importance of teamwork and commitment. We weren't allowed to miss any practice or rehearsal because each person's part was important. We had to work the rest of our schedule around this time commitment.

It took so much practice to get really good at singing together. We had to know every word, harmony, dynamic, tempo, phrasing, and cue to every song. We had to listen well to everyone's part and the teacher's instruction. I thought the amazing part was since all members came together as a whole to sing in harmony, no one's voice really stood out unless it was a solo part of the song. For most of the parts, we had to blend our voices together. Also, there were no musical instruments because it was *a Capella*. Our voices were the musical instruments to make the chords, the harmony of the notes. We had to allocate time to practice in order to hit the right notes while singing the correct verse and producing pleasing sounds. The more we practiced, the more our voices blended nicely and smoothly. We persevered to give our best. It was a combination of hard work, focus, attention to detail, persistence, and resilience - almost like sports.

That year our choir group was doing so well with our performances that we were able to raise enough money to tour Southern California schools. This was the first time in high school I traveled with a school group for a long trip

167

without one of my parents or a church youth group. I guess you can call it my rite of passage. My great efforts truly paid off.

I found the Southern California lifestyle quite party friendly with its warm spring weather. Our host teenager invited us to go with her friends to a party that first night. After checking out the scene for a bit, we weren't comfortable with that kind of party. A couple of friends and I excused ourselves and escaped the party.

Being typical high schoolers we didn't want to wait for our ride back. We walked about two hours back to the host family's house. The way back was long, but not boring. Along the path, I found it fascinating that kids were playing hockey in a covered parking garage. I never saw that anywhere in Oregon. I was awed by the myriad of lights of the big city, coming from a tiny town of 18,000 people, as we walked down from the hilly neighborhood.

Since I was not used to walking such a long distance, after a while my left leg lost its ability to walk. I tried to walk slower but my leg gave out. I had to tell my friends the truth. It was very humbling for me to admit that I had this weakness. It was kind of not fair. People could have other weaknesses that they could become better with practice, such as with sports or learning abilities. I had built my core and upper arms to become stronger, but my leg would collapse at times and my strong leg would miss a step sometimes when compensating. I was always active, so asking for help was very difficult. I never even wanted to ask people to slow down for me.

From time to time throughout my whole life, I could see people noticing my gait when I walked. There were also some who insulted me with looks of contempt and unkind words. Sometimes they stared for a long time, whether purposely or they just weren't being sensitive. I tried to ignore them, but when that happened too often, my mind would remember the way the mom in Michigan mocked me. She would tell me to climb up the stairs, and while I was going up, she'd have a mirror in her hands and say heartlessly, "Walk straight! Why can't you walk normally?"

But both my friends were nice. They offered to give me a piggyback ride. At first I didn't want to, since I felt embarrassed and small to be so needy. After a while, I relented. They were sincere. They knew I was uncomfortable, so they made it fun by taking turns and making stories as they carried me. What true friends they were.

Along the way, by God's grace, we found an abandoned shopping cart. That must have been God's providence. I didn't even pray for it, but God provided, at the right time and the right place. So, I hopped inside while my friends pushed me part of the way, not paying too much attention to the click-clackety sounds of the wheels rolling against the pavement.

To protect me from feeling ashamed, my kind friends never told the story to the remaining choir group. It was a weakness I had to deal with all my life. Sometimes I could ignore it, but other times I had such anguish in my heart. I believed God wanted me to surrender my brokenness to Him. I didn't want to have self-pity so I just kept asking Him how to delight in my weakness, in insults, in hardships, in persecutions, and in difficulties. I asked Him how to make sense when the Bible said, "For when I am weak, then I am strong."©

Maybe He was teaching me. I still didn't quite get the lesson, but I believed Him enough to know that He wanted to heal my brokenness.

CHAPTER

13

High School Senior Year

...so that you may approve the things that are excellent, in order to be sincere and blameless until the day of Christ;
Philippians 1: 10

13.1 Anchored

Therefore, my beloved brethren, be steadfast, immovable, always abounding in the work of the Lord, knowing that your toil is not in vain in the Lord.
I Corinthians 15:58

In 1981, the Roseburg High School football team, the Indians, under legendary head coach Thurman Bell, made history by winning the highest league's AAA State Championship. The exceptionally strong team, who were mainly seniors, finished unbeaten with a 14-0 record and were the first Oregon prep team to win 14 games in a season. Thurman Bell continued to lead the team into three more championships during his glorious 45-year career as a head coach.

My pastor, Pastor Dick, invited me to watch the state championship game in Portland. That was the first time I went to Portland to watch any game. It was about three hours from home. It was a memorable night watching the game with him and especially to be able to celebrate the sweet victory right there in the stadium.

That special moment with Pastor Dick made an impression in my heart. It gave me a good start to twelfth grade, encouraging me to run my race like an athlete and not look back. I decided to become more committed to God and to seek Him in all decisions in my life.

Twelfth grade was also when I became fond of Keith Green's songs. I still liked those hopeless romantic pop songs, but they didn't minister to my soul. I didn't listen to those songs anymore. I wanted to be close to God. Keith Green's songs came at the right time. They were so prophetic, moving, anointed, and full of the truth.

For example, every time I sang, *Oh Lord, You're Beautiful©*, I truly could worship and turn the lyrics into sincere prayer. And I would be in tears, knowing His eyes are on this child (me).

Some people even compared him with the Old Testament prophet Ezekiel because he would sing about the loose morals and weak faith of our generation. I enjoyed all his songs. It might feel funny to some, but I felt like

I was being mentored by Keith through his songs. They anchored my faith like no other songs.

About a month after my high school graduation, on July 28, 1982, Keith Green died in a plane crash along with 11 other passengers and the pilot. Green was with two of his children, three-year-old Josiah and two-year-old Bethany. His wife Melody was at home with one-year-old Rebekah and was six weeks pregnant with their fourth child, Rachel, who was born in March 1983. It was so devastating to everyone in the Christian world, including myself. I grieved because I lost such a powerful musician who made an impact in my spiritual walk through his songs and ministry. Even right now, when I feel down, I go to his songs and worship. Oh, how they lift my soul.

13.2 College Decisions

"David, have you thought of what you want to study in college?" My dad asked since I just started my senior year in high school.

"I don't know for sure yet, Dad, maybe engineering or computer science," I replied.

He nodded. "You're quite good at math, so I suggest you take engineering or accounting. Either one of these professions will give you a good career, son."

"Yes, I'm not too keen at taking a business major, and engineering sounds like something I'd like." I didn't want to say engineering sounded way cooler to me. Then I added, "Computer science is what everyone is talking about too. They say it's booming. Programming is the way of the future." I still wasn't sure which one I should choose.

"Son, I have prayed about this and talked with your mom for quite some time. We both agreed to supply all your financing to finish college."

I hugged my dad and later my mom. My dad kept working until I finished college. Later on, I found out he took out an insurance policy to pay any of his debt to make sure it covered my college expenses. They truly supported my dream.

I prepared to go to college by taking college classes in high school, about 30 credits. Going to college was a natural next step, maybe since all my friends were doing it, however, I didn't know I was supposed to prepare for the college entrance test called the SAT (Scholastic Aptitude Test). Praise the Lord, although I didn't get a very high score on that test, it was good enough to enter any state university, like Oregon State University.

At my graduation, I was 11th out of 500 in my senior class. I received several awards like The National Scholars Award and was inducted into The National Honor Society. Like others who were bound for college, I received tons of university literature in the mail beckoning me to apply to their universities. Most of them were from out of state mid-level universities.

I prayed and thought hard and came down to three options: Boston University, General Motors Institute of Technology, and Oregon State University. (OSU). Since I wanted to stay close to home, I wanted to go to OSU, but my brother-in-law convinced me to go to the local Umpqua Community College (UCC) and transfer later to the university. UCC is located at Winchester, just north of Roseburg, where we lived. It offered strong technical programs in both computer science and engineering, among other majors. It sounded like a good option.

Sharing from his personal experience, my brother-in-law elaborated on the advantages of going to UCC first. The first two years would be easier, then I could transfer into the professional engineering program at Oregon State University. I looked up to him, so I listened to his advice. Besides, I needed to be considerate of my dad's sacrifice. Going to UCC for the first two years would save him a lot of money. I could always find a part-time job for my allowance and living cost.

Now that which college I'd attend had been decided, I just needed to have confirmation from the Lord about my major. If I took engineering, then which field? And how about computer science?

One day I was looking at a brochure from OSU for different kinds of engineering programs. My eyes went to a slogan under the mechanical engineering program that said, "Turning Ideas Into Reality." That did it. A mechanical engineer I would be. That may not be the best method to decide upon a major, but I was naive.

I wasn't the first to get a chance to go to college, but I was the first to receive a university degree. My dad had won a scholarship to MIT in his youth, but instead he chose to get a job to earn money. As a veteran of WWII, having served in the Asian Theater, a job was more important after the war. One of my sisters had taken some classes at the local community college. From what I know, for the Pearman line of ancestry, I would be the first to achieve a university degree.

CHAPTER

14

First In My Family

Unless the Lord builds the house,
They labor in vain who build it;
Psalm 127: 1a

14.1 First College Friends - Asians!

Beloved, let us love one another, for love is from God; and everyone who loves is born of God and knows God. The one who does not love does not know God, for God is love.
1 John 4:7-8

In high school, as I said, there were only a handful of Asians, but I tried to avoid all of them. I knew them generally, but I just never talked to them personally because I didn't want to be associated with them. The main reason was, subconsciously I wanted to make a distinction between myself and them. These Asian kids had Asian parents, so they were "full Asian." Barry Liu was born in Roseburg but had Chinese parents who came as immigrants. Keiko Tanaka was born in Japan, and she moved here with her parents and older sister. Sam Heng, who was a year above me, came from Cambodia. Lastly, Ken Kobayashi, a Japanese exchange student, lived with an American host family.

I expected people to see that my case was different. Yes, I was adopted, yes, I looked Asian, but I had American parents. So, I wasn't Asian American and "full Asian" like they were. In my eyes, I was "whiter" than they were.

I wasn't being racist, but I just didn't know how to process the lingering issue that defined my identity. I wanted to block out my Korean past, so when I encountered other Asians, I would sometimes avoid them out of my own shame—shame of my past, cultural ignorance, and inferiority for being an "outcast" Asian.

When I was younger, my parents tried to connect me with the other Korean adoptees through different events that Holt's organization would hold in Oregon. They were willing to travel and take me, but I always rejected their invitations since I didn't know how to embrace my Korean identity while trying to grow my American identity. My wise parents never wanted my adoption to erase my race, my background, and my opportunity to have some kind of Korean experience, even if I couldn't have it to the full extent. They knew I wasn't on board about connecting myself with the fellow adoptees. They didn't know the real reason, and I wasn't clear about it either.

I had a secret wish that I wanted to be white, and not Korean, not Asian. My face and my body looked Asian, but my blood and flesh, the way I talked, and the way I thought were American. I was only attracted to white girls and the majority of my friends, if not all, were white. When I went with my family to large family reunions, I didn't even notice that everyone else in the room was white except me. They were all family, so I never felt left out, invisible, or different.

But the Lord saw that what I was doing; not accepting who I fully was would not be good for me in the short or long term. I didn't realize I was holding on to hurt by trying to bury the hurt instead of dealing with it. So, He gave me a surprise.

The first week in college, God put in my path a few Asians who were in the community. They became my very first friends. I started attending the International Students Club for some reason. I met Tak, a boy from Japan, Chhor and Hak, two refugees from Cambodia, and Suresh and Hiran from Sri Lanka. I helped some of them with writing since English was their second language and college writing was difficult, even for me. It felt good to be needed, and they were actually great friends who were loyal and fun too.

God must have changed my heart because I was happy to be with them and wasn't afraid people would think I was an international student like they were. Somehow, that wasn't important anymore. God in His infinite wisdom knew how much their friendship would color my first two years of college and mine, theirs.

In high school, I was always eating alone, until I met Brian Fuller. In college, the first thing God taught me was that when I stretched the circle of friendship wider, where there was no wall separating the insiders and the outsiders, a powerful thing happened. Friendship happened. No one felt left out, ignored, or invisible. We could embrace any race, background, socioeconomic status, skin color, and all other differences, because love and kindness prevailed.

Then I thought of God. He wanted all people from all languages, tribes, and tongues to know Him and His love so they would not perish. God loved everyone and all people. God was an includer all along.

"Oh Lord, help me be an includer. Give me more of that love so I could just love all people, including people from my race and background," I prayed before I retired to bed at night.

14.2 Being Planted
In the House of the Lord

Those who are planted in the house of the LORD shall flourish in the courts of our God.
Psalm 92:13

Ever since that day when I earnestly asked the Lord to help me in my faith journey so I wouldn't have a yo-yo kind of faith, being planted in a Christian community was very important for me. It was actually number one on my to-do list upon arrival at college. After much praying, I attended Campus Challenge, a Christian Club that met on campus.

After the first year, Campus Challenge announced that China was opening up its doors to foreigners from America. China was closed before since it was a communist country. Now, since it was open, it was our chance to bring the gospel to them. Some families and even students responded to the call to go and take Bibles into the country. We, the students, were encouraged to go for the summer, since it was easier for singles to uproot themselves than families with children. There would be intensive training on evangelism, as well as learning Chinese cultures and some basic language skills.

Now that the Lord had changed my heart and removed my Asian shame, I actually wanted to go. I was a good student of the Bible and I knew God wanted all people, including these Chinese who didn't have any idea at all about Jesus, to know Him and be saved. God had spoken to me about that part early in my college year. So, I inquired for more information.

I learned that I had to raise support to be able to go with this organization. That was too much for me; I didn't have the boldness and courage to face people, share my vision, and then ask them to support me. I was too shy. I felt my personality wasn't cut out for this part at all. I knew there would be some people from my circle of family, friends and even church who had the means to support me, if they could see the vision of serving Christ in China, but that was a big hurdle in my eyes at the time. I struggled with that for a long time, and finally I told the coordinator that I wouldn't pursue this opportunity.

I don't know if I felt sad or relieved when the team went. Honestly, it was a mixed feeling, but the team seemed joyful, excited, and confident of the new chapter they were about to experience. I decided to support one family monthly with my small allowance. At least if I couldn't go, my money should go and help. It would represent my desire to go.

14.3 Hurdles at the Professional Engineering Program

But you, be strong and do not lose courage, for there is reward for your work."
2 Chronicles 5: 7

At UCC, I took all the baccalaureate classes and the pre-engineering classes. I also signed up for computer science classes in my freshmen year and did enjoy them. Praise the Lord, He allowed me to get basically two academic scholarships to cover my tuition and some left over for college expenses. I worked part time to have additional money for personal spending and some savings. I took jobs mainly as a tutor in math and at the library.

To transfer to the professional program from UCC to OSU, only two engineering majors were accepted: mechanical engineering and civil engineering; there was no transfer program for the computer science program. I wanted to work as soon as possible, so I applied and was readily accepted into the mechanical engineering professional program at OSU. I was getting closer to my dream of becoming a mechanical engineer, but not before I had to face some hurdles.

Yes, my brother-in-law was right about it being easier to transfer directly into the professional engineering program from a two-year college. What he didn't tell me, however, was that the work in the junior level classes was like leaping up the stairway of academia. I was used to leisurely walking up the academic stairs. It took several terms to not only get used to the rigorous work, but also how to find the right people to work together with and how to make the university system work for me.

First, when I transferred, my community college credits were transferred but not all the grades. I earned good grades with the pre-engineering classes and the baccalaureate classes, but they wouldn't take into account my 3.83 GPA. Some credits were counted, and I was grateful for that, since all the engineering classes for juniors and seniors would be much more difficult.

Second, since my OSU peers had been in the same classes from their freshman year, they already had established a good support system for their university success. They had connected with study friends. This was one of the keys to being successful in the engineering program. From studying for exams, to solving homework problems, to doing projects and labs, having study partners made everything easier and better. I was mostly studying by myself and eventually had to push myself to connect with friends for projects and labs. Finally, God gave me a friend and study partner, Dave from Albany, who transferred from another community college. It was funny that we both were transfer students who met at the heat transfer class!

Third, at Umpqua Community College, the instructors taught in small classes. They went by their first names and were very friendly and accommodating. I even played tennis with some of them, and some were advisors in the campus clubs in which I participated. I got to know them, and they also got to know me by name. Now at OSU, I wasn't used to having to make an effort to know my professors and the teaching assistants. I hardly used their office hours and other invitations from faculty to make myself known and get the help I needed. My peers had gotten to know the faculty and were used to asking for help and support. The university had prepared a support system to help students achieve their academic goals smoothly and successfully. Some examples of these were access to teaching assistants, writing centers, math centers, career services, old exams and projects to study from, but I didn't use any of these services.

When I felt like I was striving alone, the song, *When I Hear the Praises Start*© from Keith Green reminded me of God's love and all He had done for me.

183

14.4 Connecting with God's Family

And let us consider how to stimulate one another to love and good deeds, not forsaking our own assembling together, as is the habit of some, but encouraging one another; and all the more as you see the day drawing near.
Hebrews 10:24-25

It had been ingrained in me by the Holy Spirit that I needed to be planted in a spiritual family. So I searched for one, and I was blessed to have two spiritual families while I was at OSU.

After looking at some options for housing, I came upon Varsity House, a men's Christian co-op house located in Corvallis, near the OSU campus. I wanted to live with a Christian community. I was sold when I read their brochure. This was the fellowship that would foster spiritual growth and provide venues for me to serve as well. I applied and got accepted.

Immediately, I made friends and brothers with 45 other guys at Varsity House. We were so blessed to have Maxine, our motherly and joyful house mom, and Linda, our house cook, whose special chicken soup with thinly shredded chicken was the best I had ever tasted in my life. It was at Varsity House that we developed such a strong Christian brotherhood. We prayed we would help one another become men after God's own heart.

During my second year at Varsity House, I moved up to the second floor from the basement "dungeon." Actually, the dungeon was quite adequate since the entire house was freshly remodeled the summer before I came, but upgrading to the second floor was really a privilege for me. Not only was there a better choice of a room, but my friend, who was nicknamed Lambo, invited me to room with him.

The second spiritual family God provided was through a church in Corvallis. The story of how I found this church reminded me that my steps were ordained by God. I had worked as a janitor at a doctor's office during high school. Upon learning that I was going to OSU, the doctor told me about a church in Corvallis that I should check out.

I visited the church and felt the Lord wanted me to be planted there. The church centered itself around 3Cs: Christ, Church and Community. Pastor Steve was such a humble man, and he had such a shepherd's heart. The worship was passionate; I could feel the presence of God. The preaching was very biblical and pointed to Christ the whole time. And the church body was so welcoming to me. I felt at home right away.

The location was quite far from where I lived near OSU, but I didn't have a problem connecting with the church and joining all the activities. At first, all I had to do was call a number to get a ride with others. Soon I had friends from VH who would ride together. My season at the church was filled with great memories with a wonderful, caring family of believers.

During my college years, I learned from Gilbert Faxon to love the Word of God on a deeper level. Gilbert was a farmer and rancher. He served as an elder and a church trustee. He passionately taught the college Sunday School and led Bible study groups. The Holy Spirit anointed Gilbert with the gift of teaching, and as a teacher, he consumed the Scriptures as food to his heart, soul, and mind. He was a master storyteller. He would capture all of our attention as he told the stories while explaining the Scriptures passages. He wanted to dig deeper into the Word in order to know Him and then make Him known to others. His purpose in teaching was so the believers could be built up in their Christian faith so they wouldn't be swayed back and forth by wrong teachings.

Gilbert always said he was teaching never for our head knowledge, but so we all would learn and apply the truth of God's Word into our lives. He really challenged us to think deeply when we read the Bible. He had such joy and satisfaction when the Holy Spirit opened our minds, and we were able to see deeper into the truth in the Word of God.

Gilbert said when we became so hungry for His Word that we became the students of the Bible ourselves, that was his best reward. What a true teacher he was. We started our study from Genesis all the way to the New Testament. We never stopped studying. We devoured the Word together, one Sunday after another. To this day, I still remember our discussions on Genesis 1, Abraham, the Sermon on the Mount, and the Beatitudes and I pass them on to others.

Even though Gilbert Faxon did not graduate from college, he was able to enlighten us with God's Word. He was a man who loved God's Word and enjoyed teaching it to others for God's purpose and glory. Gilbert Faxon was a gift to my hungry soul and my critical mind.

14.5 Summer Fun and Being a Trendsetter

Go to the ant, O sluggard,
Observe her ways and be wise,
Proverbs 6:6

Summer was so much fun at Oregon State. I was a child when it came to playing and having fun. I didn't have any classes, so I applied for a job at the OSU main library. While I was working there, I met a guy who became a friend. We started playing Frisbee™ golf all throughout the campus on a specified, uncharted golf course.

Frisbee™ golf is a game that combines Frisbee™ and golf. The way to play it is similar to playing traditional golf. We would throw the Frisbee™ into a basket or at a target instead of using golf balls and golf clubs. The winner would be the one with the lowest score. We could have 9 or 18 targets, just like in regular golf courses.

I learned from two gigantic crewmen from Varsity House that OSU had a gorgeous Frisbee™ golf-course. It started with the two of us, but pretty soon we brought others to experience the unusual fun. After a while, we decided to expand the game. In fact, I marked on the folding campus map the course for future use and for posterity's sake. We crisscrossed the campus for two hours at a time. All summer long we played this new game.

We played "lost and found" with our Frisbees™ between green juniper bushes and sometimes inside professors' offices. One balmy summer evening, my Frisbee™ went up but we didn't see it go down. We looked all around the building and behind the bushes but still couldn't find it. I looked up and saw an open window, so we speculated that it went inside the open window. I jumped up and pulled myself up to the open window. A man, maybe a professor, came to see me and retorted, "May I help you?" I had to say, "Sorry, can you hand me that Frisbee™ behind your couch?" while trying to hang on with my arms. He graciously retrieved it for me.

Sometimes we never could recover our Frisbees™ as they disappeared onto the roof or into tree branches or thick, dark, prickly bushes. Our

Frisbees™ flew around trees, screeched through garbage can openings, whistled past building archways, flew over one cafeteria, sailed down and around the stairways, landed on top of benches, or pinged onto the stop signposts. It was a workout, but it was a blast. I was able to walk a lot because it was not fast walking. In that two-hour time, I could never get bored of seeing the beautiful trees, the various-styled buildings, and the lush green pastures all around the campus.

I introduced my church college group and many other friends to the course. I passed out the 18-hole Frisbee™ -golf maps to all of them. I wanted Frisbee™ golf to be a trend.

To a certain extent, I seemed to be a trendsetter. A trend I wanted to believe I set was holding an umbrella while riding a bicycle. It rains a lot in Corvallis, and it is not fun getting wet. For me, I hated the hassle of having to wear rain gear from home to my classes. It took time to put on and take off the gear. Where would I put the wet rain gear during class? So, I decided to use my handy foldable umbrella with the curved handle my older sister Patty had given me as I rode on my bike. Yes, I would grapple with the umbrella in my left hand while holding onto my handlebar with my right. It worked for me. I had enough leverage to go up the slight hills, and the umbrella, if properly positioned, would keep me fairly dry. I didn't get wet, and I avoided the messy rain gear.

Actually, I always had an innovator side of me. I would see a need and want to solve it. If I had the ambition, I would have designed and made a bracket to mount onto the handlebar with a transparent umbrella. That way I thought I could be safer and more stable. That invention never happened; however, I used my technique and I started seeing others do that around campus. I really don't know if it was because of my influence, or I just saw others already had the same idea.

187

14.6 Experiencing God's Mercy and Grace

Then the Lord passed by in front of him and proclaimed, 'The Lord, the Lord God, compassionate and gracious, slow to anger, and abounding in lovingkindness and truth;
Exodus 34: 6

Spring term was always a challenge for me. After burying my face in the books for fall and winter terms, I was ready for spring break—one week of break after the end of winter term. My problem was I enjoyed spring break way too much and was unmotivated to start my spring term. In engineering, the hardest classes seemed to be offered in the spring. That was the time to push yourself and finish well. I did the exact opposite. I don't know if it was because the sun was finally coming out more frequently after six months of dull, cloudy weather, or if I was just burned out from studying. When the sun came out my books closed up.

It was so humbling to see my report card that spring. I failed terribly in not only one class, but two that senior year. I had reaped what I sowed. The challenge about senior year was that many senior classes were only offered once a year. Out of the two classes I failed, one was going to be offered in the fall, so I had a chance to retake it. This meant I would delay my graduation by one term, but the other one was only available in the spring of the following year. Not only did I make terrible mistakes for not taking my classes seriously, but they also carried terrible consequences. Now I was facing the gut-wrenching risk of delaying my graduation one full year.

Of course, by this time I was in a lot of turmoil. I felt guilty for not working hard enough. I was so disappointed in myself for not planning wisely enough about my future. Then I thought about how God had provided for my study and my dream in many different ways. It was in God's favor that I was the recipient of the Longview scholarships throughout my college years. Also, my dad had kept working so he could fund some of my college expenses. I had worked at the library and also took a part-time job at Hyde and Associates Engineering. I felt I had let down God, myself, my parents, the organization who gave me scholarships, and the people who graciously gave me part-time jobs. I felt I hadn't been a good steward to all of them and to God. I had wasted their efforts by stalling my graduation.

My thoughts went into destruction mode. I couldn't help feeling like a failure. It turned out I was still basing myself as David Israel Pearman who prided myself in my winning formula of being smart, strong, independent, and not making much trouble for others. That was my identity. So, when I allowed myself to fail, I had the phrase "I am a failure" all over me.

I was at the point of giving up my future dream and career as a mechanical engineer, but then I would have wasted four years of college study. I had no simple solution. Praise the Lord. He sent one brother from Varsity House to be there beside me, encouraging and cheering me on to persevere and find hope in Him. What a treasure this brother was for being there for me when I was in the lowest valley of my life.

I pleaded with God for His mercy to be able to graduate on time without waiting for one full year. I begged God for a special favor for my meeting with the dean so he wouldn't require me to retake that one class which was only offered in the spring term. It seemed so impossible. I had asked my friends to pray for me too. I had to break my will and all the pride inside me to be transparent to them. I had been sowing bad seeds of laziness and irresponsibility each spring. Now I was about to reap the consequences. I could only turn to God for mercy and grace despite what I had sown.

When I was in the conference room waiting for the Dean of the Mechanical Engineering Department, I prayed and prayed for God's mercy and not justice. My heart beat so fast when the dean finally came into the room. He wasn't smiling so I was really nervous. I took a humble position by telling him first how sorry I was and how I had messed up my plan.

He discussed with me the options. He told me the two engineering classes I failed were required to graduate. I proposed to him to give me grace and a solution to graduate in the coming fall term. He consented that if I get a B average in the two engineering courses in the fall, then he would waive the required failed class. I happily agreed to the terms and thanked him over and over. I experienced God's mercy and grace that day.

Mercy is the act of withholding deserved punishment. In His mercy, God could have punished me by letting me suffer another year of waiting for the class. Grace is the act of endowing unmerited favor. In His grace, God gave me favor with the dean to work out a solution. If I could get a B average for all my engineering classes in the fall, then he would let me graduate.

189

How did this story end?

Here was my testimony. In the spring, the best, most helpful teacher taught the electrical fundamentals class that I had failed. I didn't open the textbook because I didn't buy one. I had borrowed one from the library, but the sun called me away from my studies. Now the worst part of this deal was that the same class would be taught in the fall by the hardest and least popular professor in the program. Everybody in his class feared this professor, and the rest avoided him like the plague.

On the first day of class, he announced proudly that half of us would fail his class. Even with these challenges, God gave me the favor to give my best effort. When I received my final report card for my four classes, I received an "A" for this electrical class and "C" for the other required design class. This was a "B" average! I was thanking God up and down the hallway.

The LORD proved Himself merciful and gracious, slow to anger, and abounding in steadfast love and faithfulness in my life through this painful but redemptive life lesson.

I was able to see that when I failed my winning formula, it worked against me. It attacked my identity by marking me a failure instead of just failing. When I relied on God's grace, my identity in God remained the same. He forgave me and helped me get a second chance. There was a distinct difference between the convictions from God that always built up versus the condemnations from Satan that always tore down.

14.7 Roommates at the House on 29th Street

A friend loves at all times,
And a brother is born for adversity.
Proverbs 17: 17

The summer before I graduated, Lambo, my roommate from Varsity House, planned to move to the house of his friend. He talked to Lortz, Fleming, and me to see if we wanted to move in together. We all had been living at Varsity House and it was time to move on. When Fleming and Lortz graduated, they found jobs in other cities. We found Morgan to replace them. After Lambo found a job in Washington, and Morgan graduated, I found Eric and Junichi to room together. Then Junichi transferred to a college in Northern Washington, so I drove him up and bid my farewell. So finally we added our final roommate name David. To avoid the confusion, he chose to be called David and I remained to be called Dave, so that settled that.

I immediately found Arif, my friend from Somalia, who was working on his undergraduate studies in electrical engineering to be roommates. We even took on the challenge of being the apartment managers with about 50 apartments. That was an agreement we would regret. After several months, we hardly wanted to answer the phone, since we knew it would be another complaint. The $100 discount on the rent was not worth it. After three months we quit to save our sanity.

The next year Jack, a PhD candidate and a friend from Nicaragua, moved in with us. All three of us, jokingly nicknamed ourselves The Three Musketeers. We were more like The Three-Stooges instead from the old comedy show. We would chase each other around inside this apartment with whatever we got our hands on to throw at each other and then vice-versa until we would laugh each other silly. Sometimes we had to do something crazy to break the monotony of everyday living together. One time in our horse-play we knocked down the only plant I owned, - an arm-sized, easy-to-take-of, potted plant which was given to me in honor of my father. The whole plant, dirt and all, came flying out of the pot. I stopped for a moment to

191

gingerly deposit the remains back into the pot. Despite the many abuses, the plant amazingly survived through another year.

We had very deep discussions about life, about God, about marriage, and about the future. We often joked we would be "bachelors 'till rapture".

Arif and I would be roommates for the longest years. To this day, Arif and Jack are the roommates I have kept in touch with.

CHAPTER

15

The Early Engineering Days

The steps of a man are established by the Lord,
And He delights in his way.
Psalm 37:23

15.1 Pursuing
My Dream as an Engineer

Then the Lord answered me and said,
'Record the vision
And inscribe it on tablets,
That the one who reads it may run.'
Habakkuk 2: 2

After I graduated from the university, I worked full- time at Hyde and Associates Engineering, a small engineering consultant firm, at which I had interned part-time for over a year while finishing up my classes. Since I completed all my classes in the fall term, I didn't come back to go through the commencement ceremony which was held once a year in June. It was not important to me. I only knew a few of the classmates in that graduating class and it was a long wait to come back for a graduation ceremony I had no excitement for.

My parents were already proud of me that I was the first in the Pearman line to graduate from college. That was enough. Now I just wanted to focus on work. Of course, I interviewed with several big companies and some multinational companies, but I preferred small companies where I could make a bigger impact and get my hands dirty on all aspects of the work. I didn't want to work on a project for several years that designed the best oxygen mask on an airplane. Most of my graduating class got offers from a giant airplane manufacturing company. I didn't want to be a tiny cog in the huge machine of a company. From early on I was fascinated with how a small organization grew to a giant one that impacted the world. I wanted to be part of something that would someday directly impact the world.

Again the Lord graciously gave me a boss who was also like a father and a mentor to me. I started as an engineer-in-training under him and later became his right-hand man. His engineering office had employed three other engineers before I came on board.

Our expertise was in finding energy efficiency problems and solutions for all kinds of facilities: government buildings, schools, hotels, manufacturing companies, hospitals, offices, theaters, malls, gas plants, apartments, etc. We had contracts through the Oregon Department of Energy to do a lot of energy studies in all kinds of buildings all over the state of Oregon. These facilities would apply to the Department of Energy for these studies and that was how we got the contracts. So, Paul Hyde and I went everywhere together. We even drove to Washington and northern California to do studies as requested. Sometimes we only did the engineering study, but other times we also did the implementations where we hired the contractors to work on them with our recommendations.

We would start with troubleshooting the problems. We analyzed the issues in heating, cooling, or any other energy systems. After we looked at all the energy usages, HVACs and anything that used energy, we made calculations to estimate the budget and time required for the systems to get repaired by inserting new technology, or by designing a new one. We created a prototype or model of how the system would be installed or repaired, so we could measure and know the result. We also made heat exchangers and sold heat exchangers for waste-water treatment plants all over America.

Paul was very smart but had such an untidy desk! My OCD traits came to the rescue. I asked permission to organize his desk. He had a decent filing system but once he took something out, he just put it on his desk. He had piles and piles of books, engineering magazines, all kinds of reference books that were as thick as the yellow pages, leaving very little space to write. When I was done, he was so happy, and I was so relieved.

15.2 A Special Bond God Ordained

Therefore be merciful, as your Father also is merciful.
Luke 6:36

Back in the early 90s, computers never turned off in some buildings. Computers were new enough that there was still some fear for new users. They were afraid that if they turned the computers off, it would interrupt an in-progress disk write and cause major loss of data. Another reason many people left them on was because it took so long to reboot them in the morning.

We were at this one insurance building to do a study and give a recommendation. They had a lot of people working for them, and they each had a computer on their desk. Right away, we knew that they could save a lot of money by just turning off the computers at night. Computers back then generated an amazing amount of heat. We calculated by turning off the computers, the company would save up to $30,000/year. That was a lot of money back then. They just had to put up with the two minutes of turning them on in the morning. And we hadn't even looked at other energy sources.

We went to hotels, big and mid-size, to save them on their energy bills. For hotels, we needed to monitor hot water usage because that would be one of the places to save energy. In one particular hotel, we did the study and had plumbers install the equipment. Prior to that, I made a program to monitor the equipment and schedule the frequency of the monitoring. That day, something wasn't working. I suspected it was one of the sensors, but since the plumbers weren't around, I tried to fix the sensors by myself. Before I could do anything, water came gushing out like a torrential flood. Everything became wet. I couldn't find the valve to turn off the water. Finally, I was able to turn it off. The manager scolded me badly. I was glad it happened on a concrete floor, but water was already everywhere.

The manager stormed, "You have to clean this up."

I reported the incident to Paul who was at his office. I'd never forget his calming voice on the other line. Rather than blaming or rebuking me, Paul said, "Dave, would you want me to drive over and help you clean up?" Oh, he was so fatherly. What a gentle, kind, and comforting boss the Lord had given me. The two of us dried the room together for several hours.

15.3 A Surprise Purchase at God's Kairos Time

When the time is right, I, the Lord, will make it happen.
Isaiah 60: 22

Although I didn't have a car yet, I had learned how to drive. In fact, I already furnished myself with a driver's license, with the help of Troy, my generous and kind friend. Troy had cerebral palsy (CP), so his 10-year-old Volvo™ was definitely safe to drive. It had a knob mounted on the steering wheel so Troy could turn the wheel easily. Troy would sit in the passenger seat patiently to support and guide me as I got comfortable navigating his car for several weeks. Before I took the test, I spied at the driving test. Troy and I followed around someone who was taking the test to see what they did, not knowing that my test would follow the same, exact path. Yes, I finally received my precious driver's license after seven years of waiting for the moment. Troy and I both rejoiced. I respected Troy for his tenacity and wit, and for being a faithful support in my life.

Not long after that, Troy tied the knot with his beloved wife who also had CP. The day they got married was one of my happiest for another person when his wife walked down the aisle on crouches to the tune *The Rose*© by Bette Midler. Ever since then, I fell in love with that song because of the warm memories with Troy.

The first year in the 29th Street house I couldn't afford to buy a car yet, so I got myself a Honda Spree from a guy at the Varsity House to be able to get around. And did I go everywhere on that small scooter! It would only go 25 mph unless I was going downhill then I could push 30mph. Sometimes I had to visit the office on Highway 35 which was a 55-mph zone. I still dared to go out on that highway, but I drove on the side shoulder.

Since the 29th Street house only had a dryer but no washer, I dumped the clothes in a tall, dark, plastic garbage bin and hauled it on the Spree. I had installed a blue milk crate on the back of the Spree with bungee cords to carry some goods. It was the obvious place to secure my clothes bin, or so I thought. Going to the nearest laundromat was fine, and I was able to balance out the weight.

After washing the clothes, I forgot the laws of physics. My clothes were wet now and so weighed immensely more than they had when I brought them. When I revved up the accelerator of the Spree, suddenly my front end sprang up and in a moment's time I was sprawled on the ground with my Spree, my dark brown laundry bin, and yes, my clothes. Thankfully, the wet clothes were still secure and saved inside the bin, but it didn't save me from the embarrassment of the public eye. After I recovered and composed myself, I readjusted my vehicle, respected the power of balance and leverage, and sped cautiously home. That didn't stop me from using my Spree to go everywhere.

I dreamed of one day buying my own car. I had been working for 11 months, and I had saved up some money. It was a long Thanksgiving weekend, and my friend dropped me in Roseburg. For some reason, I told my dad about the Spree incident with the laundry, and he suggested we go down to the car dealer and look for a suitable car. What?

I couldn't believe it. I fell in love with a silver, Honda™ Civic hatchback with metallic red stripes on the sides. It was beautiful. The three-year payment plan worked out with my budget, and my credit checked out with my dad as co-signer. Wow, my first car! I was so proud as I drove up to the house to show Mom. My mom couldn't believe her eyes. I called my friend in Grants Pass not to not pick me up since I was now a proud owner of "Silver Bullet" as I christened it. During the entire two-hour drive back to Corvallis, I was still glowing with pride. My legs and arms were tired from driving for so long, but I enjoyed every minute of it.

God knew what was best for me. He generously gave me the desire of my heart when the timing was right in His eyes. That was the first time I learned that God had His *Kairos* time. *Kairos* is different from *Chronos*, which is a regular time that is ticking all the time. The word *Kairos* is a Greek word which means "opportunity' or "fitting time". God's Kairos moment is God's appointed time to act. When it is His timing to act, everything accelerates. I was glad to experience the provision of a car in His way and at His timing. I would cherish this testimony for the years to come every time I needed provisions from Him.

15.4 Praying for a Wife

Then the Lord God said, "It is not good for the man to be alone; I will make him a helper suitable for him."
Genesis 2:18

One October day in 1987, when my mom was visiting me from Roseburg, she noticed I was not my happy self. I confessed my longing to Mom: I had already graduated and was working in my career, but I had no young lady to share my life with. She then bluntly asked "What do you want in a wife?"

I hesitated a second.

"Mom, do you remember the one time I went with you to a Holt gathering, something I had always refused?"

Mom nodded. Still, I needed to remind her what happened.

"Okay. So if you remember, at that Holt Adoption gathering, there were many Korean adoptees like I was. And yes, I know I should have been mingling with them but I was still awkward at this and I saw they were too. They were with their families.

"And you were so bold, Mom, wanting to help God find me a wife. You asked a young Korean lady nearby, 'Hi Miss! Are you still single?' to which she graciously replied, 'Hi. No, I am not,' pointing to a man a few yards from us. 'My husband is over there.' I was so embarrassed and later on I reprimanded you saying, 'Mom, do you remember what happened when Sarah tried to help God to get a son for Abraham through Hagar? You were doing just that today!' You apologized but I was already a victim of your boldness."

Mom laughed and said, "Sorry, son! I know sometimes I put my foot in my mouth. Yes, that was embarrassing, although now we get a good chuckle from it." She added, "Okay, so, what do you want to have in a wife? This time I will just be praying. I won't do anything, unless the Holy Spirit tells me to."

"Haha, that's okay, Mom. I know you didn't mean it, and I know you will be careful this time. I have been reading several books about marriage and relationships. So, my conclusion is I am looking for a GOIA woman."

"A *what* kind of woman?" Mom was confused.

"A GOIA woman. GOIA is godly, outgoing, intelligent, and attractive which I adopted from a book I read."

"Oh, wow. That's so good," said Mom, who then asked, "Anything else?"

I added, "Well, yes. I would like my future wife to love kids, play the piano, and one more thing. You might laugh at this, Mom. She needs to be shorter than I am." That really limited the choices, but I would feel comfortable if I was taller than my wife.

After I relinquished my wish list, my mom responded, "I will start praying for this."

After some time passed from this conversation with my mom, there was a Filipino girl to whom I was attracted. My mom helped me pray, but nothing happened, although she seemed to respond to my friendship. Another time, I had become close to a Singaporean girl. Again, my mom and I prayed for God's will, but she had to move.

These short possibilities opened my dad's eyes that if I married an Asian spouse then I might have to move somewhere far to follow the girl. He was sad because it meant he would risk losing me. Then he said he had to give me to the Lord. As parents, he and Mom were just stewards of me. I belonged to God. So he was sad but would be happy for me. I felt the love from my dad when he expressed that.

15.5 My Dad's Passing

...for if we live, we live for the Lord, or if we die, we die for the Lord; therefore whether we live or die, we are the Lord's.
Romans 14: 8

"David, how are you? Dad will have surgery on Tuesday, the 21st of July," Mom said on the phone.

"Oh Mom, is Dad okay?" I was worried, knowing Dad had fought type 1 diabetes for many years and had been having to take shots.

"Yes, it's his diabetes. Dad has worked his way down from taking shots to consuming pills only, but unfortunately, he still has problems with circulation in his legs, so the doctor suggested surgery," Mom explained.

"Oh Mom, should I come and visit him?" I started making plans.

"Oh son, you're so caring. I'm sure your visit will brighten his spirits. Please be praying and don't worry." Mom assured me.

"David, don't be so concerned. The doctor has said the risks are minimal, and he has done many of these before. I just need the blood flow in my legs to circulate better," Dad suddenly took the phone from my mom.

"Okay, Dad. I'll be praying. I think I can come the weekend before your surgery. What do you want for your 60th birthday? It's just one week from your surgery," I said while looking at the calendar.

"Oh, son, your visit would be a gift to me already," Dad said before we said our goodbyes.

That weekend I drove to see my dad. We spent the whole Saturday hanging out. It was mellow and relaxing. We reminisced about a lot of funny tales from his childhood. We had a hearty laugh together.

Sunday we just stayed at home. We didn't want Dad to be too tired. We turned on CBN and sang along to some of the praise and worship songs after breakfast. Then we rested. Dad had to be admitted on Sunday evening to prepare for the operation early Tuesday morning. We went in, and got my dad settled. He joked with us and with the nurses, just being witty. Everything was fine. I had to get back to work on Monday. We prayed for God's favor for surgery, and I hugged him goodbye.

Monday, I worked but my mind was on my dad all day. I prayed for the surgery, also for peace for him, Mom, and for myself.

Early Tuesday morning I woke up and prayed, "Father, please pour out Your anointing on the surgeon and all the medical staff who are taking part in the surgery for my dad. Lord, help Dad feel Your presence and fill his mind and heart with Your peace and joy and faith in You. I pray for a smooth and successful surgery, Lord, and a fast and successful recovery. Bless all who are helping him, Lord, and help them to know You. We ask in Your Mighty Name, Jesus."

Then I went to work.

"Hyde and Associates Engineering," I answered the phone. It was 8 am. I was already at work, organizing for the whole week's projects and tasks.

"David, Praise God. The surgery went really well. Dad is still in the recovery room being watched," Mom almost shouted.

"Oh Mom! Praise the Lord. I had been praying," I replied happily.

"Got to go. Love you, son." Mom said and hung up.

"Thank You, Lord," I whispered.

At 10 am Mom called me at Hyde Engineering.

She was crying, "David, Dad just passed away…"

I was in total shock. She said he came out of the surgery well and even joked with the nurses. Then two hours later, he suddenly and unexpectedly had heart complications and he was gone to be with the Lord face to face. Two days ago, my dad was laughing and joking with me, and now he was gone.

I was quiet, trying to register this great pain of the loss of the one man I loved most in my life. His birthday was the coming Tuesday. He was turning 60 years old. He was taken from us, too early for our timing, but the Good Lord had decided.

After my dad's passing, Mom and both my sisters were quite peaceful. In fact, Mom wanted to have a joyful celebration of Dad's life and said, "I don't want a stranger to walk by the memorial service and start mourning too." So we had a very merry celebration of Dad's graduation to Heaven. It was a beautiful ceremony by Pastor Dick Halaas. We all shared precious moments, funny anecdotes, and treasured lessons from Dad. I didn't shed any tears. I didn't mean to, but maybe my winning formula had taken over. I didn't try to act strong. Or maybe I was trying to be joyful, knowing the hope I had in Jesus that one day we would be united again in Heaven.

For months and even years later, I really missed him during my young adult years. I regretted his early departure. It pained me that I never did get to ask him some important questions about courting and finding a wife, and about marriage and the relationship after marriage. He would never know my wife and my children someday. He would have been such a loving father-in-law and such a fun and kind grandfather.

One day when we were rummaging through all his stuff in his shop and study place, I found a yellow ruled paper folded up in his study Bible. It was a note to me.

My dad had written,

My son, it has been wonderful to watch you grow from a 'little kid' to a great young man. I could write a thousand words and not tell how much I love you, so I want you to know, 'I love you'.

Protect your mother as a good son should but never, never let go of Jesus Christ! He can make your life beautiful if you let Him. Love everyone you meet and be forgiving when the world hurts you. Jesus will hold you close when you need it.

'Fried Chicken' will have to wait till I see you in Heaven.

Love Dad.

Tears ran down my face as I read it. I hugged the precious yellow paper to my chest. "Fried chicken" was our game when I had just been adopted, as I said earlier. I felt the pang of emptiness as I looked around in his shop.

"Dad, I wish you were still here with your smile and wit. How can I manage life without you mentoring me with your advice? Dad, you'll always be my hero. Did you know how much I love you and look up to you? I still do, not did.

"Dad, thank you for loving me so much. I know you sacrificed greatly to support my dream. When you were supposed to retire and enjoy your life, you promised to continue working to help me with college expenses. And you kept your promise. I know you were struggling with your heart and diabetes, but you persisted to stay alive to see me graduate and work as an engineer.

"Dad, I miss you more than words could say. You were such a good earthly father that it was easy for me to know my heavenly Father's love too."

I was sobbing now.

15.6 Being Involved in the International Ministry

Go, therefore, and make disciples of all the nations, baptizing them in the name of the Father and the Son and the Holy Spirit, teaching them to follow all that I commanded you; and behold, I am with you always, to the end of the age."
Matthew 28: 19-20

When I arrived in Corvallis, my friend Tak invited me to an international Bible study at Papa Don's. Papa and Mama Don were missionaries to Africa for many years. When they returned to the States, they started ministering to international students in the area. So, I went with Tak and some others to North Albany to join Papa and Mama Don.

I immediately loved the fun and friendly atmosphere at that fellowship. I kept coming every week, but Tak never joined again. After many years, this fellowship closed down. A new fellowship to Indonesian students was formed with Albert and Reba along with Papa Don and Mama Don. Of course, I naturally jumped to help with that ministry.

I didn't know much about Indonesia, except that when I was in fifth-grade, I did a report on the Krakatoa volcano eruption in 1883. Krakatoa was part of Indonesia. This eruption was famous because it began on May 20th and peaked on May 27th, destroying 70% of the island and its surrounding archipelago.

It turned out my new Indonesian friends knew much less about Krakatoa than I did, but they appreciated the fact that I did a report on part of their country. That was how friendly, kind, and inclusive these Indonesians were to me. As I could see their sincerity, I felt very much at home with them. Yes, there were times when they joked among themselves. They used Indonesian and they'd laugh so heartily, forgetting that I didn't understand their language. But I was fine and wasn't offended even a bit. I knew some jokes couldn't be easily translated to English because they wouldn't be as funny.

These Indonesians took turns cooking meals. I began to know different foods and the word *sambal* which meant hot sauce. Sambal was hotter than tabasco. They put sambal on anything. I couldn't handle much spiciness, but the food was always nice. Soon a yellow turmeric chicken soup called *soto ayam*, a dark beef soup called *rawon*, beef in coconut milk called *rendang*, chicken curry called *kare ayam*, and fried rice called *nasi goreng* became my favorites.

One day, Papa Don told Albert, Reba, and me that a family from Texas was coming to check out the ministry to international students in Corvallis. He wanted us to have lunch with them to promote that they should move to Corvallis. The day came and since the Lyalls liked Mexican food, we went to a popular chain restaurant that served that type of cuisine. If there was a better Mexican restaurant in Corvallis, we didn't know of it.

Don and Claudelle came with their three beautiful grade school aged daughters: Bonnie, Becky, and Beth. I remembered their names because it was mathematical. Their names were, six, five, and four characters long. I guess our strategy and welcoming hospitality worked. They packed their belongings and moved the following year to Corvallis.

CHAPTER

16

Becoming the Right Person

Do not conform to the pattern of this world, but be transformed by the renewing of your mind. Then you will be able to test and approve what God's will is - His good, pleasing and perfect will.
Romans 12:2

16.1 The Baggage

Therefore, since we have so great a cloud of witnesses surrounding us, let us also lay aside every encumbrance and the sin which so easily entangles us, and let us run with endurance the race that is set before us,
Hebrews 12: 1

I still was carrying around emotional baggage which was deeply packed within my heart. Physically, I still owned and carried my lone plaid bag wherever I moved. It was old and torn up. I had covered my name given by the Michigan family and my Korean name with a black marker, but for some reason I had never gotten rid of it.

That plaid bag was a symbol of my internal emotional baggage. Yes, with my own "marker", my set of winning formulae, I attempted to erase my past, both as Juhn Joong Ki in Korea, going from one house to another to the Holt Orphanage, and as David Israel Johns with the first adopted family in Michigan.

After I became a Christian and grew in His truth, I was full of joy and hope of what He had prepared for me, but I was always focusing on what the future held for me and never was free in talking about the past. I didn't see the need to go back to the past. I was probably subconsciously protecting myself from being hurt if I opened myself up to others about my past. People only needed to know I was adopted from Korea, and that was it. Now I was this American man named David Pearman. That was what I portrayed.

In my memory, my past was locked in a box and the box was sealed in a chest. The chest was buried in the bottom of the abyss that I didn't want to locate anymore. I had thrown away the key to it forever. I didn't know this wasn't healthy all along. More important, I didn't know this was a sign of unforgiveness that the devil could use as a foothold in my life.

One day I was having lunch with Don Lyall and the subject of my past came up. He asked, "Dave, how did you get adopted? I want to hear your story."

I was caught off guard. I muttered, "Oh, my parents always wanted to adopt a Korean baby, and so I was matched with them."

I could tell he wanted more details, but I had never shared my whole story with anyone. So far, people just knew that I was adopted and that was sufficient. They also didn't inquire more than that. On top of this self-guarding, I didn't want people to have pity on me, and I certainly didn't want to harbor any self-pity in myself. This was probably my winning formula trying to dominate me again, but I was not conscious of it.

I thought we weren't supposed to dwell in the past anyway, like the Bible said about forgetting what is behind and straining toward what is ahead in Philippians 3:13.

So, Don's question startled me a little. He asked, "Dave, have you ever wanted to know your birth family?"

"No, not really," I said. "I mean, I'm happy and grateful to be adopted by my parents." It sounded good. It was the truth. I was truly happy and blessed to be living as the son of my parents, as a Pearman. It felt like I would be betraying them and their kindness if I still had "troubles" or "heaviness" over my past. Or so I thought. Another truth was I didn't want to dig up my past that I had buried so well.

"Oh, okay. Do you want to visit Korea someday and see the orphanage?"

"I don't know, Don. Honestly, I don't have any interest in doing that."

"Oh yeah? Why is that?" he probed. "It seems you like hanging out with the Indonesians, and any Asian students here in our ministry."

"Well, actually I didn't want to hang out with Asian kids when I was growing up. Then in college I started having Asian buddies. When I began working, I got to know Papa and Mama Don and Albert and Reba. So, I wasn't always hanging out with Asians," I opened up a little bit.

I could tell he knew I was uncomfortable. He patted my shoulder and then walked away.

The next time I met with Don Lyall, he asked if I had a second to talk to him. We went to the kitchen area of his house away from the crowd. I could tell he was very thoughtful and careful at conveying what he wanted to say to me, so I prepared to listen. He said something that was very profound.

"Dave, have you considered talking to a Christian counselor about your past? Even for us, people from a regular family, not adopted, we could still be carrying baggage from the past.

"Don't get me wrong. I mean, you don't seem to be free to share about your past. It may mean there might be some hurts and pains you have been burying. Or maybe not. I could be wrong. I don't know. But if you did have some baggage, it would surely come to the surface in the future. Maybe seeing a counselor could help you see something God actually wanted to set free.

"I know you desire to be married someday. I think it's a good idea to deal with all the baggage you might have, so if God brings you a partner for life, it will be easier in the marriage. Maybe you can pray about it." He tapped my shoulder and walked to the living room where all the Indonesians had been waiting.

Don didn't know for sure, but I knew for sure he was right. I was carrying a lot of baggage over my past. I couldn't know the reason why, but my mom said I was a sensitive child and got my feelings hurt quite easily. Besides, I had been working now for several years. I was really thinking about the future and had started longing for a wife.

So, I took Don's advice to pray about it. The more I prayed about it, the more I could see the need to meet with a Christian counselor.

16.2 The Path of Pain to the Path of Forgiveness

Whenever you stand praying, forgive, if you have anything against anyone, so that your Father who is in heaven will also forgive you your transgressions.
Mark 11: 25

My counselor was a godly and wise man. The Lord anointed him to unlock me. Upon meeting him for the first time, and talking with him, right away I felt connected with him. I felt I could trust him. He didn't come with a preconceived idea about me. He just directed the conversations as they would develop.

He had questions that made me ponder deeply what happened. He was able to show me different issues I had from my past, way before my first adoption.

I did realize this about myself: I was never free at talking about my past. I didn't know what to do about my past. I was just burying it deep, suppressing everything since I couldn't make sense out of it. I just thought the past should stay in the past; I didn't think it was a form of unresolved trauma.

I didn't think I had an issue, like I harbored some kind of hate or feeling of revenge. I really didn't, but my past was affecting me in countless invisible ways, and I wasn't aware of this at all. This was my blind spot that no one ever mentioned.

My counselor was patient with my process, which made me feel at ease with him. He stayed, listened attentively, asked questions, and took notes. It took many months for him to listen to me going over my life from birth to the present.

His explanations made sense regarding how I processed my feelings and thoughts and behaved as a way to protect my fragile heart.

Below are some of his explanations:

In my attempt to "forget and let go," I had this unresolved trauma that I didn't realize was haunting me and directing the way I acted relationally and the way I processed everything. Old wounds that I tried to bury were giving me psychological effects that triggered certain reactions in me. For example, I always thought I wanted to look and sound American because I was living with my adopted family. But if I was truly healed, I would not have rejected the Korean identity in me. I would have wanted to know more about Korea or my childhood upbringing. I must have felt shame, abandonment, rejection, loss, being unwanted, or even fear of whether more negative emotions would come up if I dared myself to think about my past, let alone search upon it.

If I was truly healed, I would have had no issues sitting with other Asian kids during my school years or befriending them. Instead, I didn't want to be associated with them. Subconsciously, being associated with them opened up my wounds of the past.

If I was truly healed, I would have given grace to myself for having polio. Instead, I tried hard to compensate for that disadvantage by hiding behind my winning formula. I reckoned I always had a feeling of shame when people looked at my legs, or when they stared at my gait.

If I was truly healed, I would have had no problem sharing my stories that were actually full of testimonies of God's hand in my life. Instead, I hid my stories and only talked about the present and the future.

After such a long process, my counselor was able to help me identify exactly what I had buried all these years behind my tough stance: the issues of loss, rejection, shame, guilt, grief, identity, insecurity, the desire to control by means of my winning formula, and even the fear of intimacy.

So, my problems weren't just because I was abused and rejected by the Michigan family.

Now about that wound.

My counselor gingerly probed into the most painful part of my past: what happened in Michigan.

"David, you didn't know how to deal with your trauma in that Michigan home, how that family treated you. You haven't made sense of what happened. Not only have you been traumatized and scarred by the abuse, but you have taken blame for it, leaving you with a feeling of shame that you think you deserve. Therefore, you always feel guilty and shameful about it. You feel you were wrong about what happened.

"One of the ways to resolve this unresolved trauma is to create a coherent narrative. What truly happened? Let's walk through it together. Let's create a coherent narrative together. "

We looked at my timeline on the table and walked through each story.

"So David, what you experienced was abuse. That's right. Anyone who heard your story would agree with me that they were abusing you. The whole family, and especially the mom. Did you hear me, David? You were not to blame. They abused you. She abused you.

"This is why for so long you just couldn't make sense of it. You didn't have a name for it. You couldn't process your own feelings about it.

"So, the new narrative, the truth is, that she abused you and Jesus rescued you from her grip so that you would know Him and have a better life with the Pearmans."

Now with the new narrative, I was able to see how different the reality was from the one I had accepted and had continued to believe since I was a kid.

Next, my counselor helped me to see that all the above baggage came from having so much bitterness that I had buried. The key to having the freedom from these issues was to allow God's love to flow through me so I could forgive.

So, he gently and caringly helped me walk through my past. I had to open that path again. I had closed the door, buried, and covered it with my own strength. This time, with Jesus holding my hands, I could do it. It was the path of pain before, but now, it was the path of forgiveness.

16.3 Walking With
Jesus in the Path of Forgiveness

For if you forgive others for their transgressions, your heavenly
Father will also forgive you.
Matthew 6: 14

I had to walk in a path of forgiveness with Jesus.

First of all, I had to learn to forgive my birth parents. They had the best intentions to give me away, especially my birth mother, since she wanted a better life for me. She probably couldn't take care of me. The Korean societal norm would have made a mockery of her and me, since single mothers were looked down upon, especially having a child out of wedlock. Whether my biological dad knew or not that he created me with my biological mother, God in His infinite wisdom ordained that I was to be born, to fulfill His calling in my life. I was born for His purpose, and not for the purpose of my parents. And even if I was created in sin like from a rape, an affair, or them being intimate before marriage, God in His sovereignty had allowed me to be born. He was the Master of turning something from ashes to glory.

I forgave my mom and my dad and said a prayer for them to be saved if they didn't know Jesus yet. As I forgave them, I also released the negative feelings I harbored because I was given away. Namely, the loss and grief of not knowing them, the rejection, being unwanted and not worth anything. I thanked God that I was, above all, His child. He indeed had known me even before I was in the womb. He kept me safe since He knew I would know Him, and He would consecrate me so I could walk in His path for His purpose and glory.

I had to forgive my first and second foster families. The first foster family was the only family I knew at that tender age of three to six years old. Of course, my Halmoni and Hal-abeoji, the "grandparents," had no choice but to let me go to another family. They no longer had the ability to take care of me. My heart used to ache whenever I remembered this was the place I experienced such agonizing pain that I vowed I would never allow my feelings to be hurt again. I was too young to remember my birth parents or how I was in the baby home, but this was my first pain.

I forgave them and released my loss, grief, rejection, and sense of identity and belonging that were robbed so abruptly from me when I had to move out of the house into another foster family. I had tears, but now they were tears of freedom. I no longer ached thinking about the "grandparents."

For the second family and shack home where I contracted polio, I had to forgive them for they gave me the best they had. It wasn't their fault I was disabled in my left leg. Polio just happened since I was not vaccinated early enough to have the complete doses. As I forgave them, I released my loss and grief over not being able to walk normally and not being able to play sports, something I would have been good at. I had to release the pain I tried to ignore every time I saw people judging me or even their concerned looks when I walked, and the insecurities that plagued me at times about whether a girl would marry me someday.

I had tears over this path of forgiveness. It was a mixture of painful tears from visiting that path, but walking with Jesus and giving forgiveness truly freed me like the counselor had said.

But I still had a long way to go.

"Jesus, give me strength," I prayed.

My counselor always knew when to stop and continue the next session. Each session really was an eye opener and a breakthrough for me. We would work on my first adopted family next, which took many sessions to unlock what really happened.

Then the hardest part.

I had to forgive the Michigan family for the child abuse. I had a list of what happened and prayed for forgiveness over each. The counselor suggested I write a letter; whether I mailed it or not was my choice.

So, I prayed to God for guidance on how to write this letter.

Dear .... and ....,

I hope this letter finds you well.

My name is David Israel Pearman. You might or might not recognize my name, but in 1971 you adopted me into your family. It didn't work between us, so I was put into an orphanage temporarily and then was adopted by another family after a few months of being there.

The Pearman family has loved me and considered me their own son since the first day I got there. They also helped me know Jesus, so I accepted Him as my Lord and Savior. Jesus has changed my life forever for the better. I now live for His purpose and glory. So, I am doing really well. I have graduated from university and have been working for a few years now as a mechanical engineer.

I am writing to let you know that I have forgiven you for all the physical and emotional abuses you did to me. Jesus helped me go through a path of forgiveness so that I could be free from all hurts, bitterness, hatred, and any negative feelings.

I hope you also consider Jesus to be your Lord and Savior, if you haven't. He loves you so much and in Him there is love, joy, peace, forgiveness, and grace. He is the Way, the Truth, and the Life. Knowing Him will change your life forever too.

Humbly submitted,

Dave.

I didn't mail that letter, since, for one, I didn't know if the address I had was correct. Second, I had already declared my forgiveness and just the act of writing that letter set me free from the bitterness.

I had to forgive God, and I had to forgive myself. Maybe, secretly and subconsciously I blamed God for giving me such a childhood. I wondered what my life would have been like if I never contracted polio. What if God had healed me? Just like Apostle Paul, I asked at least three times to be healed. I needed to forgive God for having me go through those horrible times. But as Romans 8:28 tells us, God "works out all things for good to those who love Him, to those who are called according to His purpose." God knew those trying times would mold my character to be more like Him by causing me to focus my eyes on Him.

In the end of the counseling sessions, for the first time in my life I was able to verbally forgive all, including myself. But it may take a lifetime to keep forgiving for seventy times seven.

I did feel the weight getting lighter and lighter, and that I finally would run freely with endurance the race God had set before me.

16.4 Empowered To Obey and Be Bold

Therefore, my beloved brethren, be steadfast, immovable, always abounding in the work of the Lord, knowing that your toil is not in vain in the Lord.
I Corinthians 15:58

A few months later, my boss and I had a long drive for a new project. Paul and I took turns driving but mostly he did. To kill time, we talked about all kinds of topics from the newest HVAC systems in the magazines; to the newest computer, Macintosh™ by Apple; to the time when he was in San Francisco experiencing an earthquake while he was talking with me as I was housesitting his house in Oregon, and back full circle to the recent engineering problems and solutions we just tackled.

Then at one point, Paul started sharing a bit about growing up in La Grande, Oregon. Suddenly the Holy Spirit nudged my spirit, *Share your testimony with Paul.*

What, Lord? Is this really from You? Even after going through months of sessions of healing with my counselor, I still hadn't opened up to others. Not to anyone, not even to my own mom, nor my childhood pastors, nor the young adults in Farmer Gilbert's Bible study, nor new friends in the ministry like Albert and Papa Don. No one in the past and in the current time ever dared to ask, except Don Lyall, for the sake of being polite and sensitive to me. So, no one ever knew my story.

My counselor was the only one who knew my whole story, and he was bound by counselor-client confidentiality, so I was safe at sharing.

Besides, it was honestly quite emotionally draining going through the childhood pains with my counselor. I was grateful to walk the path of forgiveness. But I just couldn't share again. My story was too long, and too complicated. What was the purpose of sharing? I guess in my mind, it was the past and it was already over. Before, I had wanted to forget the past and had learned to survive with my winning formula. I had protected myself from other people's pity and my own self-pity if they knew my story. So that was

217

wrong. Now, my reason for not sharing was right on: it was the past and I was healed now. So, could I just move on? Move forward? Besides, Isaiah 43: 18-19 says "Forget the former things; do not dwell on the past. See, I am doing a new thing! Now it springs up; do you not perceive it? I am making a way in the desert and streams in the wasteland."

The Holy Spirit broke my arguments in my head. *Yes, Dave, you need to share. You need to plant the seed of faith in him now. Tell your story.* The Holy Spirit was clear but gentle like in Jeremiah 23:28, "Let My true messengers faithfully proclaim My every word…. Does not My word burn like fire?"

Lord, You know this is my boss, I said silently. *I don't want to get into trouble. I might offend him and lose my job. And it may not be professional.* I tried to evade this calling to evangelize. But the more I tried to suppress it, the more it was burning like a fire within my soul. I became so fidgety in my seat. *Lord, can't I just practice first by telling my mom first? And Don Lyall?* I tried to bargain.

My heart was beating so hard. I was restless and antsy like a five-year-old boy. My hands were clammy. It felt as if my passenger seat were burning hot. I couldn't stand it anymore. I had to obey!

"Paul… (I took a breath). Did you know that I was adopted?" I started, while at the same time praying, *God, please lead me in this conversation and give me a favor to share.*

"To be honest, I had that thought, David, but I didn't want to ask and cause you to be uncomfortable." Paul's response was so reassuring.

So I went ahead and shared my story, from Korea at a baby home to having a few foster homes, how I got polio, when I was in the Korean orphanage, how I was adopted by the Michigan family that didn't work out, and finally about my dad's dream that was a confirmation for my parents, the Pearmans, to adopt me.

I talked about how God had given me peace over all that happened and that I was able to forgive everyone, by God's help and strength. And I needed to do that for myself too, to move forward with Him.

He was teary when I was done. I was too. It was so good for me to share my story. It was my first time ever to share, and I felt such true freedom and goodness of God flowing in me from being obedient to Him. God knew I needed to do that for Paul's sake to know Him, and for my sake as sharing my testimony felt so powerful, like a seal of His healing process for me.

That Christmas, I gave him one of the greatest devotionals, *My Utmost For His Highest©*, by Oswald Chambers (2007, Logos). Dorothy, his wife, told me that he read the devotional often if not every day. Since then, he became tender to God and the things of God.

16.5. Freed to Love and be Loved

Then the Lord God said, "It is not good that the man should be alone; I will make him a helper fit for him."
Genesis 2:18

Ever since I started allowing Jesus to come and heal the brokenness of my past, I had been able to pray for things I had never prayed for before. For example, I never wanted to know my birth parents, but now I prayed for them. And not only that, I also prayed over myself to cut off any generational issues passed down from my birth family. Jesus died for generational curses in my family, so I didn't have to own them.

I started to wonder about my physical, genetic, and emotional dispositions. First, I looked in the mirror and accepted my Korean identity. I was blessed with all the good qualities coming from my Korean heritage. Maybe my math brain was from my birth dad or mom. I was also quite athletic, despite the physical effects of polio. Maybe that was genetics too. I became appreciative of the experiences in the foster homes and at the Holt Orphanage that made me a very neat, hygienic, organized, and systematic person. Since I had no sugar or candies in my childhood and never got accustomed to the taste of cola or soda, my teeth were strong and protected. I never had cavities in my life.

All in all, I was made in the image of God. As a child of God, I asked the Holy Spirit to transform me into the character of Jesus, as He was and would always be what I needed to become.

Second, the Holy Spirit continued to help me identify my feelings. Before, it all was a mixture of feelings. Meeting with the counselor helped me identify whether I was feeling abandonment, rejection, loss, grief, fear of losing control or whatever it was. These were real but buried deep and never dealt with. Now I could pray for freedom in those areas so they could be replaced and set free with God's truth.

One of the strong issues was the fear of rejection. I had to admit that I struggled with rejection the most. For example, when I was in a group, I wanted to talk, but when I talked and no one seemed to consider my thoughts or suggestions, I felt left out and rejected. I liked to help, but when my help was not noticed, I felt more rejected than other people would. I felt they were rejecting me as a person, and it made me either sad or mad. God helped me realize that I felt that way because of my trauma of being rejected all my life as a person, until I met the Pearmans. I didn't know I had a trauma of being rejected. So my breakthrough was to be able to see that if people disagreed with me or declined my help, they were just rejecting my idea or help and not rejecting me as a person. That truth gave me freedom.

I could see the fear of rejection had crippled me in seeking closer relationships with friends, and in pursuing a girl when it came to asking her to consider dating. I was okay with making friends but to go deeper than that, the fear of rejection would play in the back of my mind. I wondered if I had, to some degree, a feeling of inferiority from having polio, being adopted, being Korean, and even being not the "ideal height." I thought too much of these things that unwittingly raised a level of insecurity and inferiority in me.

A long time ago, my mom had said to me, "It will take a special young lady with the heart of God to love you and see you beyond your polio, David. And if it is God's will, there will be that kind of girl for you. It's not how tall, how slim, how muscular, how smart, where you're from, and how much money you make. You are a godly young man. You are kind and thoughtful. You love and obey God. You are a responsible and capable young man. You are worth loving. Dad and I just wanted you to know that. And you know how much we love you and are so proud of you."

I was ready to move on. If God ever gave me a wife, I was now more prepared. God helped me get rid of my past baggage so I could move into healing. I didn't want the fear of rejection to cripple me again. I did want to be married, but it would take an amazing long process.

16.6 Meeting My Future Wife

So do not fear; you are more valuable than many sparrows.
Matthew 10: 31

God didn't answer this GOIA prayer right away, but He did answer it after many years' journey. I met my future wife-to-be, four and half years later. After my breakthrough, one thing I received from God was a new boldness to ask someone for a date if they were interested. In the past, I liked many girls before but never dared to ask. This too was a learning experience. What I didn't know until recently was that my wife had accepted Jesus into her life about nine months after my mom started praying for my future wife. She has a wonderful story of her accepting Jesus into her life on a bus going to a high school retreat.

Even to guide me to this point in my life, God was watching over me every gentle step of the way. He truly is a loving Father who watches the birds of the air to care for them when they fall to the ground. How much more He cares for me, one of His beloved children created in His image. I have experienced His care my entire life. This is the One whom I have believed and persuaded from my experience that He is truly able to keep me in His eye and all that I have committed until that final day. Just like that melodious hymn, His eye is truly on the sparrow, and I know He watches me.

CHAPTER

17

Seventy Times Seven

"Then Peter came and said to Him, 'Lord, how often shall my brother sin against me and I forgive him? Up to seven times?' Jesus said to him, 'I do not say to you, up to seven times, but up to seventy times seven.'"
Matthew 18:21-22

17.1 Forgiveness Over and Over

Bearing with one another, and forgiving each other, whoever has a complaint against anyone; just as the Lord forgave you, so also should you.
Colossians 3: 13

[**Authors' Note**: **Warning:** Chapter 17 has some graphic stories of the abuses that I endured in the Michigan home.]

After my counseling sessions, I felt like the things that were buried inside became more and more clear. As a child, I had always thought I must have made a terrible mistake that caused the family in Michigan to reject me, but I didn't know what it was. I finally understood what they did were forms of abuse.

So, I went through a strange phase. Prior to knowing I was abused, because I suppressed everything that happened with my winning formula of being smart, strong, independent, and a problem solver, I had become a tough person. But then I became so tough that I realized it was hard for me to be merciful to others. *I thought I had it tougher than you, so I expected you to stand up and survive.* In other words, since I didn't want to be seen as weak in front of others, I didn't want others to be weak either. I had little compassion for them.

Second, justice and being right were extremely important to me, so I would get very angry if these things were taken from me. *My rights in the past were taken from me, so don't you dare take my rights from me again.* This included my right to be right. If I was right and wasn't acknowledged for it, I would get bitter. Or, when something wrong was done to me or to someone else, it was very difficult for me to overcome the anger. I might even feel some hatred toward the injustice. When I helped others, I focused on "fixing" people and "fixing" problems and when they didn't work, I got frustrated. I got angry. I felt I had to fight it. Many times I felt the world stank, and I just wanted to go to Heaven.

The rejection issue continued to linger in my adult life. I struggled with anger especially. When I felt I already went the extra mile to be kind and considerate or be giving and generous, but I received very little appreciation or gratitude, I had yet to learn to serve or give without expecting anything in return. This came down to loving unconditionally. I wanted to be acknowledged for my acts of love, kindness, generosity, help, smartness or whatever it was. I was disappointed very easily and if I harbored it, I would become angry or disappointed. It was driven by the deep pain of rejection.

I didn't know all the negative feelings of rejection, feeling less compassionate, and feeling anger beyond righteous anger for injustice originated from my unforgiveness toward the Michigan family.

When God made everything clear to me about my abuse, it was very profound. I had to learn to forgive them again and again, or I would not be set free from these resulting behaviors. As I was dealing with these heart issues, He showed me each incident, what each meant to Him, and how He wanted me to forgive them for each abuse they subjected me to.

The first and major one was how the mom accused me of something I didn't do. Out of the blue, she stormed at me and stripped me naked. Not only did I feel confused and terrified, but she also made me feel the shame of nakedness. I was cold, ashamed, and afraid. I cried and begged for her forgiveness without understanding what made her so mad. I was then punished by holding heavy paint cans, while standing on a paint can. My arms soon became weary, but the fear of her being angrier kept them upholding the cans.

"Where were You, Jesus, at that moment? If You were truly my protector, why did You let this happen to me? I always thought it was my fault. But now I knew this was a form of physical, emotional, and mental abuse. Even if I made a mistake, I didn't deserve to be treated this way," I inquired.

The answer came almost immediately. I could see Jesus was there all along. I saw in His face that it pained Him to see me being abused. Then I was reminded that the Holy Spirit reminded me of His Name in my desperation. I saw myself being taken outside, still naked, and cold, as the mom yelled, "Go back to where you came from!" I saw a long driveway that would go to the road. I wanted to put myself in the bag and stay there so when the father arrived from work he would have pity and take me in. But then from my spirit I cried out His Name, "Jesus!"

And then I saw the Holy Spirit put a message in my father Don Pearman's dream because my cry went to Heaven to Abba Father. He was by the river and saw a child floating in the river. In that dream, God told him to rescue that child. He knew he and my mom were supposed to adopt a child from Korea.

That was profound. Thank You, Lord, for showing me that You were there for me, and Your eyes truly were on this sparrow, this child.

But I was not done. Sometimes, some forgiveness was meant to be done over and over, until it was truly finished.

17.2 Forgive, for They Don't Know What They Are Doing

But Jesus was saying, "Father, forgive them; for they do not know what they are doing."
Luke 23: 34a

Not long after that abuse in the basement, came the emotional abuse. At the time I didn't know it would be called emotional abuse, or even sexual abuse for that matter.

For many days, the kids had been talking about Halloween. I didn't know what it was about, but I knew it was exciting. The TV showed costumes that were available in the local drug stores. The masks looked scary to me, but the kids giggled so much every time they saw them. But the mom said she would make some and buy some, and there would be a "surprise." I knew the word "surprise" must be very special, because she had a big smile, and the kids became more excited.

When the day was getting closer, I saw the neighborhood was decorated with candles, lamps, and scary decorations. I felt eerie about them, but I kept on observing the kids' excitement.

The mom came home from shopping. She pulled out a bunch of yellow boxes. Each box consisted of a sleeveless, vinyl piece of clothing and a plastic mask that was supposed to fit over someone's face, secured on by a single, thin rubber band. First, it was a black witch or goblin's costume for the oldest sister. The second box was a costume of a TV character that I didn't remember, but it was for the second sister. The next box had a princess costume for the youngest sister. The mom prepared a cowboy costume for Billy.

The synthetic odor from these boxes was very strong and gave me a slight headache right away. The kids tried the masks on, and even put on one for me. I could feel the edges of the eye holes. They were sharp and uncomfortable on my eyes. The thin rubber band also snapped if you weren't careful when you took it off of your head.

Then the oldest sister asked, "Mom, what's for David? Did you remember him?"

That was when the mom pulled a frilly dress out of a bag. It was pink with white lace overlay. It had flowers and butterflies on it. It came with stockings that went all the way to the tummy. From another bag, she pulled out a pair of flat pointy shoes, and a crown.

The oldest sister asked again, "Is that for me, Mom? Or for Alice?"

Then the mom said, "It's for David!" and laughed so much. She kept on laughing.

The kids started yelling, "Mom, that's for a girl. It's a tutu ballerina dress! Is it for Alice? For Mary?"

The mom grabbed my hand and put the dress in front of me. She said, "Look. This will be the best costume for David!"

I cried and cried, "No!" I couldn't understand everything everyone said, but I knew this was for a girl and I was a boy. I was 10. I knew the difference between a girl and a boy. I already knew the distinction that a boy wore pants and shorts, and a girl wore skirts and dresses.

I kept crying and said between my sobs, "This!" pointing to Billy's cowboy outfit. The mom got mad. "That's for Billy! Billy! You will have to wear this tutu, David."

That evening the father came home, and the kids took turns telling him what happened. I was still crying. I heard the father and the mother talking louder and louder, like they were fighting. I hoped the father would have pity on me and fight for my case.

The next evening came, and the mom called me to come to her room where she forced me to put it on. First, she forced me to wear a diaper. "Mrs. Henderson was so nice to lend me this outfit. This used to belong to her daughter Susan when she was little. I don't want him to soil it in any way," she explained to her husband.

The husband said, "You know David has never had any accidents since he came to this house, and his report showed that he was toilet trained even in the orphanage in Korea. Do you really have to do that to him?"

But the mom put it on my body despite my cry of humiliation and horror. The father didn't know she had forced me to wear a diaper many times at school, although I cried and protested. Since she didn't budge, I had to obey her.

The next thing she put on me was the pair of the long stockings. Tears came running down my face and even dropped into her hands. But she didn't care. Then she put on the tutu ballerina dress and laughed so hard as she zipped the back part of the dress. Next, she prepared a wig and some bobby pins to put on my hair. After that, she put a crown on my hair. She told me to wear the flat, pointy ballet shoes.

The whole time she was giddy and ignored my cries. She dried the tears on my cheeks, not out of compassion but because she wanted to put some powder and lipstick on my face, like she did to Mary and Alice. But the father said, "It's enough, I said," and she took her hand away.

"Fine!" she yelled and pushed me out of her room.

The whole evening was a torture for me. The mom drove us in the station wagon to a housing complex since our house was in the country. We went from one house to another, saying trick or treat and getting candies. All the kids were laughing, and the neighbors and their kids all laughed at me. But I sobbed the whole time, first with sounds and later on just warm tears flowing down my face. I was so humiliated and embarrassed with each house we visited. I wondered if some were sorry for me. It seemed some were because they touched my shoulders in such a caring way. I couldn't wait for the night to be over. I wished I could disappear from the earth. I walked with my limp gait and tried to be strong, obedient, and to persevere.

That night the father and mother had a very long argument. Their voices were loud, all the way to our rooms.

I couldn't remember how many more sleeps after that Halloween night that the father told me that I wouldn't be their son anymore. While waiting for the new family, I would be put in an orphanage in town.

"David, you - will - go - to - another - family." He spoke slowly, so I would understand.

I understood that much English and knew it was a good thing. I knew it meant I wouldn't be in this family anymore. I was relieved. Even going up and down the stairs was a traumatic thing for me because the mom would taunt me with a mirror. I felt sick to my stomach when I looked at the stairs each day, and add to that the memories of the basement and Halloween incidents. This house was full of hate and meanness to me. I thought I had to behave well so they would accept me, but they were meaner and meaner to me.

"Yes," I said.

The father, with his gentle eyes, told me, "Mr. David Kim from Korea will pick you up." He choked a little.

He hugged me tightly with his big hands. I hugged him back.

Upon hearing Mr. David Kim's name, I felt such peace and joy in my heart. I felt good for the first time again. I thought I lost him forever and was stuck with this family, but Mr. David Kim was going to take me back and make everything better again.

After that decision, the mom and the siblings seemed kinder to me. She never apologized to me about everything that happened, but she stopped asking me to wear a diaper to school and didn't taunt me anymore about the way I walked up and down the stairs.

Shortly after, the mom drove me to an orphanage in a nearby city in Michigan. This was around late November. I would stay there until another family would be ready to adopt me. I didn't know how long, but I was happy and felt safer in the orphanage than in that house.

It would take another month before the Pearmans would be my family.

Mr. David Kim wrote to the Pearmans before Christmas time:

Dear Donald and Claudine Pearman,

I know you are on the waiting list for a baby boy in Korea. We tried to match you with a four-year-old boy in Korea, but you graciously refused. But I'd like you to inform you that here in Michigan there is a ten-year-old boy who is longing to be adopted by a godly and loving family. He just went through a difficult situation with the first adopted family. It didn't work out, and we'd love to connect you both together. I'm happy to tell you that he is one of the most pleasant and kindest boys I've ever known in my years of being the guardian at the Holt Orphanage. I hope you would consider adopting him.

I look forward to hearing from you.

Sincerely,

David Kim

He also made a personal call after Christmas. This time, the Holy Spirit convinced the Pearmans that I was the child they were supposed to adopt, not a baby. The Holy Spirit showed my mom how she had "conceived me" with the desire to adopt for 10 years, and I was 10. Holt processed my documents and in January I was in the loving home of the Pearmans.

I understood this part, but I still had to process with God about these difficult "humiliations" with the Michigan family. They were so traumatic that I didn't want to "go there."

"God, You want me to forgive what the Michigan mom did to me. I had to forgive the siblings and the father for not standing up for me. How could

I be like Jesus, who said the most profound words in the entire Bible: in Luke 23:34 'Father, forgive them, for they don't know what they are doing.'"

"Yes, Jesus, when You hung on the cross, You saw before You the crowd who cheered at Your suffering. You who had no sin, who were dying the worst kind of death punishment, for the sins of those who hated You, who plotted to kill You, asked Your Father in Heaven to forgive them, for they didn't know what they were doing."

"But Jesus, this family … they knew what they were doing. Maybe the father didn't. The children didn't. They were just following the mom and wanted to please her. But for sure the mom *did* know what she was doing. She must have known she did an evil thing to me. She knew what she was doing," I said, crying to Him. "And where were You when this happened to me?" I protested.

"I was there, Son, because you know what? The mom needed to be filled with that much hate to be that extreme to you, so that you would be taken out of that house. You wanted so much to be accepted by them, especially by the mom. You wanted so much to be 'a good boy' and please them out of the desire to be accepted, so that the adoption would work. And you were at such a vulnerable age that you didn't know what you were thinking or doing.

"If you felt that there was a slight chance or a way for you to be accepted, you could have relented and compromised. If the mom had used a kind way to manipulate you to wear girls' clothes, you would eventually wear the clothes in order to gain her approval and love and to show your gratitude to her. After a while, you could be so confused with your identity. And out of trust, you could feel that you were supposed to be a girl to feel acceptance from the mom. After a while you would believe in yourself that you were a girl.

"All these abuses had to happen so fast, so extreme, one after another, so that the father couldn't stand it. In order for you to be out of that house as soon as possible.

"It was truly My way of protecting you all along, so you wouldn't fall into that trap of hate, bitterness, and the evil plan to confuse your gender identity."

Oh wow.

"Oh, Jesus, sweet, merciful Jesus," I sobbed uncontrollably. Now I realized the series of abuses was His grace to get me out of that house.

"Jesus, help me forgive them."

"Son, if you say, 'If they would show some remorse, some sorrow and repentance, then maybe I would forgive them. You are allowing bitterness, anger, and desire to rule in your heart, and you will not experience My freedom.'"

"Jesus, I choose to follow Your ways. I choose to forgive them. I mentioned each name and each act, even when they are not sorry.

"Jesus, I forgive them because You forgave my sins too. I forgive them and release all my hurts, bitterness, hatred, anger, and desire to get even so that I may receive Your freedom, peace, joy, and love. I will not let Satan take a foothold in my life because of unforgiveness."

17.3 The Devil Comes after Me, but God's Eye Is on Me

Are not two sparrows sold for a cent? And yet not one of them will fall to the ground apart from your Father. But the very hairs of your head are all numbered. So do not fear; you are more valuable than many sparrows.
Matthew 10:29 – 31

My healing came in several steps.

After the initial path of forgiveness, I was truly able to forgive. I was truly healed and freed, but after a time, the Lord wanted me to go into a deeper healing with Him. He gave me a revelation that helped me forgive to the level of "because they didn't know what they were doing". This healing was from what Jesus said in John 10:10:" The thief comes only to steal and kill and destroy. I came that they may have life and have it abundantly."

From the very beginning, there was a devil that had wanted to steal, kill, and destroy my life, every chance he could. First, he wanted to steal everything God had planned for my life. To steal all the good promises of God, so that I would be bitter with God, reject Him, and follow the devil instead. God, of course, was watching out for me, so the devil was unsuccessful. The Lord would never allow anyone, anything, and any force to take me out of His grip.

Second, not only did the devil come to steal, but also to kill. He most likely didn't want me to be born, but God made sure my birth mom didn't abort me. He helped her to be brave enough to give birth to me and caring enough to put me in a baby home, so that I would be safe and sound. God showed me that despite not knowing the details of my birth, I was never an accident. No matter how I was created, I was always created in the will of God. I mattered to God, because He was first my Abba Father, before I had a biological or adopted father. The Bible said He had known me even before I was created in the womb. He had planned for me to be born that day, because I was to carry His purpose for Him, for His glory alone.

The devil also wanted to kill my identity, my purpose, my destiny in God, my dreams, and my visions. He would have loved it if I had ended up hating

God and having a messed-up identity. He would have loved it if I had missed my purpose in God and served my own idols instead. But the Lord was always there, watching me down to the very hairs on my head. So yes, the devil didn't kill me but wounded and hurt me. However, just like the wounded sparrow that I found and nursed to health back in the Korean orphanage, God found my wounded self so He could nurture me to health.

And when I was found by Him, everything changed. It was a process, but He began to change me from the inside. He established my identity, the meaning and purpose of my life, and my destiny in Him. I no longer had the spirit of an orphan, the source of my fear of abandonment and rejection; instead, God had given me the spirit of adoption by which, with the confidence I could cry "Abba, Father" (Romans 8:14).

The third thing the devil did was to try to destroy me in every aspect of my life. The word "destroy" is from the Greek word *arolium*, meaning "*to destroy or to cause something to be ruined, wasted, trashed, devastated, and destroyed.*" I could see how he wanted me to live a devastated and ruined Christian life. To be a Christian, but be a weak, defeated Christian with a troubled story running my life, with a chip on my shoulder to control my thoughts, feelings, actions, and words. If he couldn't make me hate God for what happened with my life, then he would want me to live as a victim, to be powerless and utterly destroyed. He wanted me to be spiritually weak in faith. As if that were not enough, he also wanted to destroy me physically through polio. Not satisfied, he bombarded me with all the self-esteem issues so I would be emotionally stunted with anger, bitterness, hate, and all those negativities. Moreover, he wanted me to be a victim mentally filled with lies and trash, so I would not have the peace of God and the joy of the Lord. And lastly, he wanted me to be socially inept, fraught with isolation, rejection, abandonment, and an orphan spirit.

But God was watching me so closely and protected my faith in such a way that even when I was hard-pressed on every side, I was not crushed. I was perplexed, but not in despair; persecuted, but not forsaken; struck down, but not destroyed (2 Corinthians 4: 8-9). He seemed to allow bad things to happen in my life, but the truth is He was turning those bad things into the very tools to help me out. He did make testimonies out of my tests. Triumphs out of my trials. His messages out of my messes.

Only God could orchestrate that all along, just like what the Bible says in: Psalm 138:8 NLT

The Lord will work out His plans for my life—

for Your faithful love, O Lord, endures forever.
Don't abandon me, for You made me.

Finally, I had to rest in the understanding that there would be parts of my life that He allowed me to understand now, and some parts that He wouldn't let me figure out until I got to Heaven someday. This took faith not to demand an answer to every single thing that happened. Let me be still and let God be God. *Lord, I forgive them for they didn't know what they were doing. All the people and all the incidents that happened were just tools used by the devil to steal, kill, and destroy my life.*

Forgiveness truly was meant to be done seventy times seven.

17.4 His Eye is on You Too

*For you have not received a spirit of slavery leading to fear again,
but you have received a spirit of adoption as sons by which we
cry out, "Abba! Father!"*
Romans 8:15

I have been living in God's redeeming grace. His redemption is much greater than all the pains of my past. Because Jesus came to save my life, I have been delivered to live fully in the abundant life He has promised. I am indeed more valuable than the sparrows.

Maybe you could relate to some chapters or parts of my story. I have some questions for you:

1. Are you a sparrow, maybe injured, who is still longing to land and make your nest?
2. Do you know He is watching over you constantly, too? You are more valuable than the sparrows, as well.

No matter how your past was, the present situation you are facing, or the burden of tomorrow you are fearing, you are His child. You are not an orphan. You are not alone facing life struggles. You are His sparrow. He is watching over you. He is victorious, and He wants to guide you by His right hand if you let him. You are created for a destiny and purpose in Him. You are created to be victorious in Him. No matter what the devil tries to make you believe otherwise, the truth says Jesus loves you so much. No one is able to snatch you out of the Father's hand (John 10: 27-29).

And not only has He always watched over you, but He also wants to adopt you into His family.

Whenever people ask me whether I am adopted, I always answer, "Yes. In fact, I have been adopted not once, not twice, but three times."

First, I was adopted by the first family in Michigan, and that didn't work out.

Second, I was adopted by the Pearman family. The Pearman mom and dad took me from my dire situation and chose to become my parents by signing my papers, paying the expenses, and taking me home. I became their son. Since then, I've taken their Pearman name and that became my new identity.

Third, I was adopted into God's family. In the same way, God chose me before the foundation of the world (Ephesians 1:4). Jesus took me from my dire situations due to my sins and paid the cost by dying on the cross for me. But it was at my conversion, my decision to receive Him as my Lord and Savior, that I was adopted into His family. As an adopted child of God, I entered into a new relationship with God. Now God is my Father (1 John 3:2), and He gave me a new identity as a child of God—His child. The Holy Spirit lives inside of me, and I live for God. I have a new blessing and inheritance in Jesus as joint heirs of God's eternal riches (Romans 8:14-17).

Friends, God has chosen you, whether you know Him yet or not. Jesus died for your sins too. If you haven't accepted Jesus as your personal Lord and Savior, I hope you will do it soon. Then you can be adopted into His family and enjoy the privileges of being sons and daughters of God. Jesus said He came to give you life and life more abundantly.

My adoption story into God's family could be your adoption story too.

17.5 Forgiven People Forgive

But if you do not forgive others, then your Father will not forgive
your transgressions.
Matthew 6: 15

I cannot close this book without talking deeper about the message of forgiveness.

I'm glad you picked up this book. Maybe you've been hurt way harder than all my traumas combined. I get it. The last thing you want to hear is that you need to forgive. The pain is real. You were the victim here, and to make matters worse and most unfair, the person who did it to you may never repent or ask for your forgiveness.

Why should you forgive?

And why is Jesus so harsh? What is this idea about that I can only be forgiven as I forgive others who hurt me? What kind of justice is that? I am not the one who did the wrongs; they were.

Yes, I know we need to forgive others who hurt us, but why does it need to be connected with His forgiveness for me, my ability or chance to be forgiven by Him? It just doesn't make sense. This is a hard concept.

But that's because firstly, forgiven people forgive.

Jesus died for my sins when I didn't deserve to be forgiven. He endured the cross for me. He endured the physical pain and the agony of being separated from the Father. He was innocent. Pure. Completely blameless. Yet He willingly took my place, my punishment over my sin and rejection of Him.

Jesus was blameless, but He died for me. I wasn't even blameless, I just thought I was better than the one who inflicted pain in me. I was being most like Jesus when I forgave. Because He forgave me, I also have the power to forgive others. Oh, what power, to be more like Jesus. Oh, what freedom that is.

Forgiven people forgive.

Second, sometimes we withhold forgiveness because we see it being a gift from us for the one who inflicted the pain on us, who doesn't deserve this gift, but the beauty of forgiveness is that God in His infinite wisdom knows this is a gift we give to ourselves. This is a gift of freedom God has prepared when we walk in obedience.

I've truly experienced this freedom. Yes, forgiveness comes progressively for me, and not immediately, but with each step of forgiveness He led me to, I was able to be freer. Each time.

Now my thoughts and my spirit are free. Now I can share my life story with anyone anywhere and anytime. My story is no longer a story of a victim but a victor. My story is a story worth sharing because it is full of God's redemption work in my life.

My life could have been consumed with resentment and bitterness the older I became. I could have become an angry, bitter married man and father who was trapped in my past. Oh, it would not have been good for my wife and children. I could have turned to depression and even suicidal thoughts. I could have been that old friend or uncle who always had a "chip on his shoulder." Less joy, less peace, and not an abundant life for sure. Because I forgave that day, and then seventy times seven after that, I was able to walk with a new narrative, with Jesus writing it.

Would you like to experience the forgiveness of Jesus? If you have never asked Jesus to save you from your sins, and to be the Lord and Master of your life, then would you pray the prayer of salvation with me? That would be a good start:

"Dear Lord Jesus, I am a sinner and I need Your forgiveness. I believe You died on the cross to save me from my sins and You rose from the dead. Please come into my heart and be the Lord and Master over my life. I want to follow You and trust You. In Jesus' name, Amen."

Now let's pray for your heart to be ready to forgive.

"Dear Lord, I want to obey Your Word that says I need to forgive those who hurt me. Jesus, as You forgave me, give me power to forgive those who have wronged me. I release forgiveness to them and please fill my heart with Your freedom, peace, and joy as I do this. Jesus, even if bitterness comes up again, help me to choose forgiveness over bitterness and hate. I know I can do this with Your help. In Jesus' name, I pray, Amen."

Congratulations! You just made the best decision in your life. Now walk in His forgiveness and the new freedom of being able to forgive those who hurt you.

Epilogue

Finding My Wife

The bird also has found a house, And the swallow a nest for herself, where she may lay her young, Even Your altars, O Lord of hosts, My King and my God.
Psalm 84: 3

"So, have you told her about it?" Albert blurted, out of the blue.

"Told who about what?" I asked. There was no introduction to this new topic, and we were in the middle of talking about Cannon Beach as a possible location for our summer retreat with the Indonesian kids.

"Do you expect us to just pray, and you do nothing? I mean, we don't mind praying. It's been many months now. To be honest, Bro, sometimes you have to make a move," Albert replied.

Oh. I got it. Albert and his wife Reba had been praying for me about a particular girl that I liked at the Indonesian Christian Fellowship where we were serving together. I also told Don Lyall and my mom to pray.

Indonesian Christian Fellowship (ICF) in Corvallis, OR, led by Papa and Mama Don, ministered to international students and one of their main focus groups was for the Indonesian students who were studying at Oregon State University. We met every Saturday evening for two-and-a-half hours. It was set up like a church service. There was worship, sharing, preaching of God's Word, sometimes Bible study groups, then offering time, intercessory prayer, and finally we closed with eating together. We took turns serving. Someone would lead worship with the worship team, someone would lead the sharing time, a few people would lead the Bible study groups, and someone would lead the prayer time. We had groups cooking each week, so the loads of the ministry were shared well and in an organized manner. We also planned for outreaches, especially for Christmas, Easter and evangelistic events. We coordinated trips, retreats, and parties for birthdays, anniversaries, and graduations.

We had new people all the time.

Here was the story of the girl I asked my close friends and Mom to pray for me.

One fine Saturday in Spring 1992, a new Indonesian girl came to ICF. She was invited by her friend. At the time I was singing a solo, as a special performance for Easter. At the end of the gathering, she came to me to thank me for a lovely song. So, I said, "Thank you." Then she asked, "Are you from Singapore?" So, I told her I was not and that I was from Oregon. I didn't think much about it, but then she started coming to ICF.

At ICF, when you were new, you had to introduce yourself. So, I knew she was 19, from Surabaya, and taking industrial engineering at OSU. I could tell she was a very friendly and sweet soul. She had two jobs, which were babysitting and working at McNary Hall as a food server in the dining hall.

242

The week after that, it was my turn to lead worship. Yana, our regular keyboard player, told me that he had to pick up someone at Portland airport that Saturday. He told me Ani the new girl could play piano, so I asked her to practice together.

I found out that she didn't know most of the hymn songs. Our song books only had lyrics. She told me she was the first one in her family to be saved. She was from a Buddhist family. She was on a bus one day when her friend evangelized to her, and she received Jesus right then. She started coming to church secretly, but then her parents found out and were so upset. As a result, she wasn't allowed to go to church anymore. That was the reason she decided to study in the US, for her religious freedom, and to know Jesus deeper. Because she was in the Indonesian church for a very short time, she hadn't been able to learn hymns and other worship songs yet.

As she was sharing, she got up, tore a piece of paper from a book, took a pen from her pencil case, and then sat in front of me again.

"Dave, why don't you just sing the song? I'll listen and record the notes my way," she said.

I was puzzled by this request, but I started singing.

As I was singing, her fingers were nimble in writing numbers, like a very long code, one row after another.

67136175 / 3331123

67136175576

6622261/117121765 (she crossed the 5,) 76

and so forth….

When I was done, her fingers stopped writing too. I was amazed. I didn't understand what she was doing. What were these codes for?

Next, she asked me to sing it again, and then this time, on top of those numbers, she put chords.

Am, G, F, Em

Am, G, F,

Dm, C, Em, Em7, Am, (A)

and so forth.

Then she sat in front of the keyboard and started playing. It was so magical. I was mesmerized. Maybe other people had the same gift or even better, but I just never noticed this magical ability unfolding before my eyes like that.

243

I didn't think anything about it, until one morning while I was eating my cereal at home, I felt I heard the Holy Spirit saying, *Dave, have you noticed my daughter? She is just like what you prayed for. She is the GOIA girl you have been praying for: godly, outgoing, intelligent, and attractive. You also want someone who loves kids, can play piano, and is shorter than you. Son, I remember.*

I was shocked.

The next chapters of my life would soon unfold, and with it, their adventures, hardships, and joys. It would be a wonderful journey to tell the next chapters in a sequel. If there were a sequel, I would include the details of waiting two years for my wife Ani to say yes to me. Then waiting for another two years for Ani's parents to approve miraculously of our relationship, and thereby my mom and I flying to Surabaya, Indonesia to finally get married. The sequel would have to include Ani moving back with me after the wedding to Oregon and being blessed with an amazing and beautiful son and daughter. The story would entail after a few years of marriage of God giving a vision while I was completing MBA school to move to Indonesia to start an education center called EfeX that would impact thousands of people even up to this time of writing. And lastly, this story would have to include meeting Pastor Jeff and Liz while serving as a lay member of International Christian Assembly, Surabaya. Without Pastor Jeff, with his steady encouragement to put my story on paper, this work would not become a reality.

Yes, it would be a wonderful journey to tell the rest of the story, but for now those next chapters would have to wait. We don't know what the future holds for us. For now, we keep going forward faithfully in what God has called us to do in Indonesia. We know one thing for sure, and that is He will continue to look after us and guide as He even watches over the little sparrow.

It turned out that little sparrow that fell to the ground that day was never alone. God used all kinds of kind and generous people to help the sparrow. The sparrow was hurt but was renewed, restored, and redeemed, under the full watch of the Master.

His eye was truly on this sparrow.

About Kharis Publishing

Kharis Publishing, an imprint of Kharis Media LLC, is a leading Christian and inspirational book publisher based in Aurora, Chicago metropolitan area, Illinois. Kharis' dual mission is to give voice to under-represented writers (including women and first-time authors) and equip orphans in developing countries with literacy tools. That is why, for each book sold, the publisher channels some of the proceeds into providing books and computers for orphanages in developing countries so that these kids may learn to read, dream, and grow. For a limited time, Kharis Publishing is accepting unsolicited queries for nonfiction (Christian, self-help, memoirs, business, health and wellness) from qualified leaders, professionals, pastors, and ministers. Learn more at: https://kharispublishing.com/

Printed in the USA
CPSIA information can be obtained
at www.ICGtesting.com
CBHW070317080424
6481CB00008B/14